NURSERY
RHYME
Knits

NURSERY RHYME
Knits

Sue Locke

Trafalgar Square Publishing
NORTH POMFRET, VERMONT

© Text Sue Locke 1989
This edition text © Ward Lock Ltd and Sue Locke 1990
© Illustrations and photographs Ward Lock Ltd 1989

First published in the United States of America in 1990
by Trafalgar Square Publishing, North Pomfret, Vermont 05053.

First published in Great Britain in 1989
by Ward Lock Limited, Artillery House, Artillery Row,
London SW1P 1RT.

Designed by Anita Ruddell

Text set in Cheltenham (ITC) Light
by TJB Photosetting Ltd, Grantham, Lincs.

Illustrations by Peter Bull Art
Photography by Clive Streeter
Photo-styling by Alison Meldrum

Acknowledgements
Ward Lock would like to thank Sally and
Robert Streeter, Tom and Laura Randell, and
Lizzie and Katy King for modeling the garments.

Printed and bound in Spain by Graficas Reunidas S.A.

ISBN 0 943955 23 8

Library of Congress Catalog Card Number 89-51257

Contents

Introduction

Knitting for children is an extremely rewarding pastime. There is a tremendous amount of satisfaction to be found in creating something that's fun, original, and very wearable. As nursery rhymes are such an essential part of childhood, I have used them as the inspiration for the patterns in this book. In some cases the nursery rhyme has simply determined the color of the garment, while in others it has been the reason why stars can be found covering a dress, teddy bears marching around a garden path, and a line of dogs decorating the border of a jacket.

There is a wide variety of garments to knit, including pants, dresses, sweaters, jackets, coats, a baby-bag, all-in-one suits, socks, hats, blankets, and much more. There are twenty-four designs for children aged from newborn to six years and each one is accompanied by its own accessory. These include a hobby horse, toy boat, finger puppet, hand puppet, and soldier doll.

There are quick and easy patterns for inexperienced knitters and those wanting something in a hurry, and there are more involved patterns that take a little longer.

The aim of this book is to inspire knitters to pick up their needles and share in the pleasure of knitting something special for someone special.

EQUIPMENT

Knitting can be a very inexpensive hobby in terms of the amount of equipment that you need. A pair of needles and yarn is the minimum that you require. However, there are some useful accessories that, while not vital, will certainly make life easier for you. Aside from your straight knitting needles, which incidentally should always be kept in a cloth bag or plastic box to prevent them getting mislaid, it is worthwhile having the following:

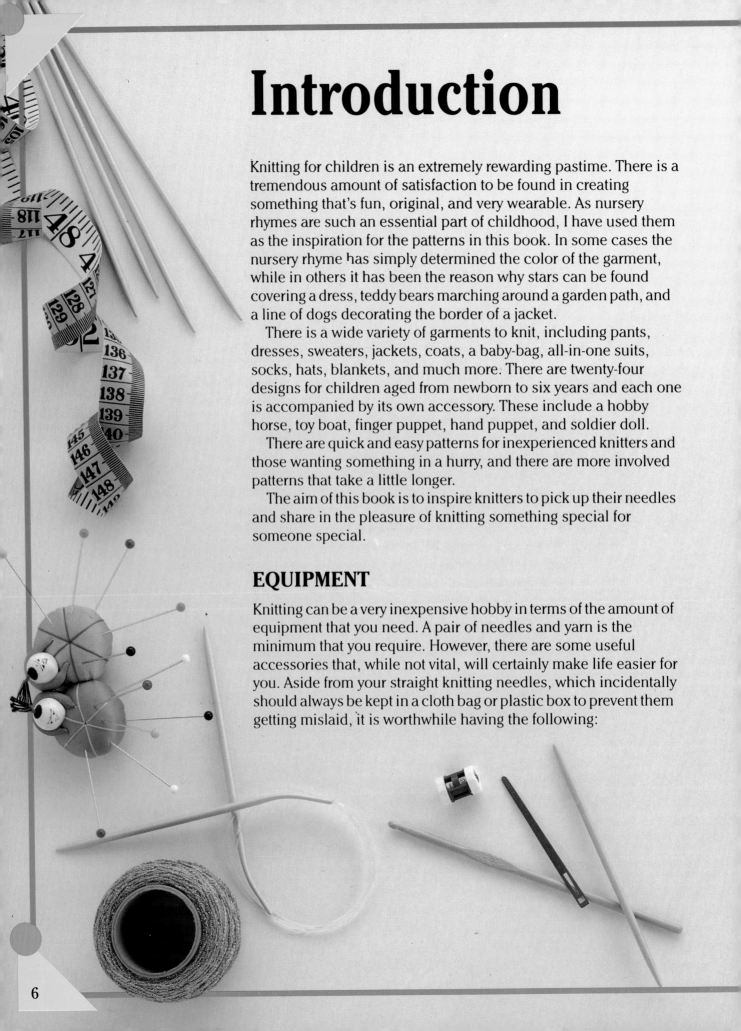

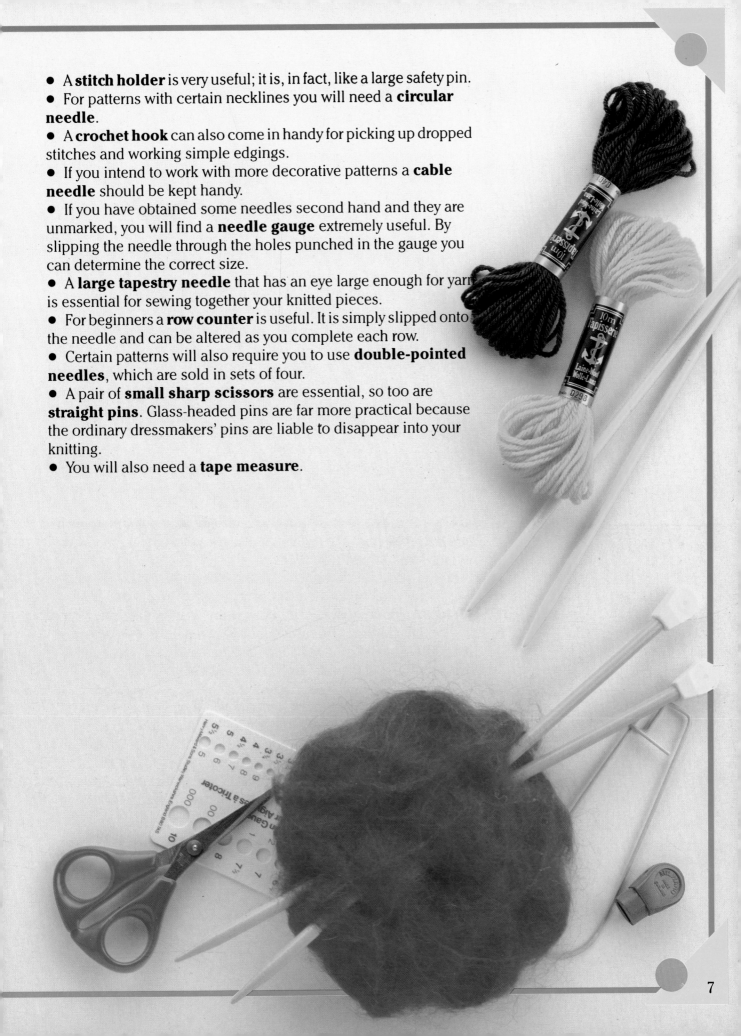

- A **stitch holder** is very useful; it is, in fact, like a large safety pin.
- For patterns with certain necklines you will need a **circular needle**.
- A **crochet hook** can also come in handy for picking up dropped stitches and working simple edgings.
- If you intend to work with more decorative patterns a **cable needle** should be kept handy.
- If you have obtained some needles second hand and they are unmarked, you will find a **needle gauge** extremely useful. By slipping the needle through the holes punched in the gauge you can determine the correct size.
- A **large tapestry needle** that has an eye large enough for yarn is essential for sewing together your knitted pieces.
- For beginners a **row counter** is useful. It is simply slipped onto the needle and can be altered as you complete each row.
- Certain patterns will also require you to use **double-pointed needles**, which are sold in sets of four.
- A pair of **small sharp scissors** are essential, so too are **straight pins**. Glass-headed pins are far more practical because the ordinary dressmakers' pins are liable to disappear into your knitting.
- You will also need a **tape measure**.

All equipment should be stored in a large bag or box. Inexpensive work bags made of fabric suspended on a wooden frame can be bought in most notions departments. It is worthwhile investing in one to keep your equipment confined to one area or there is the distinct possibility that children will cover your scissors with glue and needles might be used for unblocking sinks!

SIZES

One of the first and most important considerations to be made when making garments for children is to understand that children vary enormously in size for their age. You have only to look at a class of five-year-old's to see how much they vary in both height and width! The patterns given in this book indicate an approximate age, followed by the finished chest measurements. Check that the chest, length, and sleeve seam figures are sufficient for your child, before you start knitting.

YARN

These days the variety of yarns available is enormous. However, many yarns are not suitable for children, either because they are extremely expensive to knit with, such as silk, or because it is inadvisable to use them. Fluffy yarns are not suitable for babies as there is the likelihood they might pull at the yarn and put fibers into their mouths and swallow them.

The yarns in this book tend to fall into three categories. They are either pure wool, or a synthetic fiber, or a mixture of both. Garments in pure wool are extremely warm but are likely to be the most expensive and extra care is needed when it comes to washing them. Some pure wool yarns can be washed in a machine, but it is advisable to wash them all by hand to ensure that they retain their shape.

Yarns made from synthetic fibers such as acrylic or nylon tend to be hard-wearing, making them ideal for children. The yarn label will probably advise you to use a washing machine as this will not damage the yarn in any way. This type of yarn also has the added advantage of drying quickly unlike wool. Yarns that offer a mix of wool and synthetic fibers perhaps offer the best of both worlds with the warmth of wool and the washing advantages of the synthetic ingredients. Synthetic yarns are the cheapest, followed by the mixture of the two, with wool being the most expensive. Under the heading "Materials" we have recommended the type of yarn that should be used for a particular pattern. Where a sport yarn has been used, you can easily substitute the same type of yarn from another manufacturer, but do not be tempted to use a different weight of yarn altogether or you will not obtain the correct gauge.

GAUGE

To achieve a professional finish on any hand knitted garment, it is necessary to ensure that your gauge is correct. On the yarn label of most yarns, manufacturers usually specify the gauge to be used. Knit your gauge swatch using the needle size recommended in the instructions for each pattern. Take your swatch and pin it around the outer edges to a board, then count out the number of stitches and rows to ensure they are correct and correspond with those recommended in the pattern. If you discover on measuring that your square measures less than it should, try substituting a slightly larger needle or your garment will be too small. And if the square is too large then you should try a smaller needle or the garment will be too large. The success of a pattern hinges on correct gauge, so if you need to alter your needle size, knit your gauge swatch again to be certain that it is correct.

FINISHING

Before a garment is assembled it is usually necessary to put it through a process known as blocking and pressing. However, before pressing any garment check with the instructions on the yarn label.

Take each piece of your garment separately and pin it to a board or old table covered with felt, or a blanket or towel, and then covered with a sheet. You will probably find that an ironing board is too narrow for this purpose. To adjust the size of your garment fractionally, ease it to the size you require then pin it into position. With a warm iron and a damp cloth gently iron over the surface. As yarn is liable to stretch easily, especially when it has been ironed, it is important not to move the garment until it is quite cold. Never be tempted to use too hot an iron as you will stretch your sweater completely out of shape. Too hot an iron will also make the surface of the garment too flat and spoil the texture of the yarn. Once you have removed the garment pieces you are ready to sew them together. Use leftover yarn to sew your pieces together. On very bulky yarns separate the yarn into strands so it can be threaded easily through the tapestry needle.

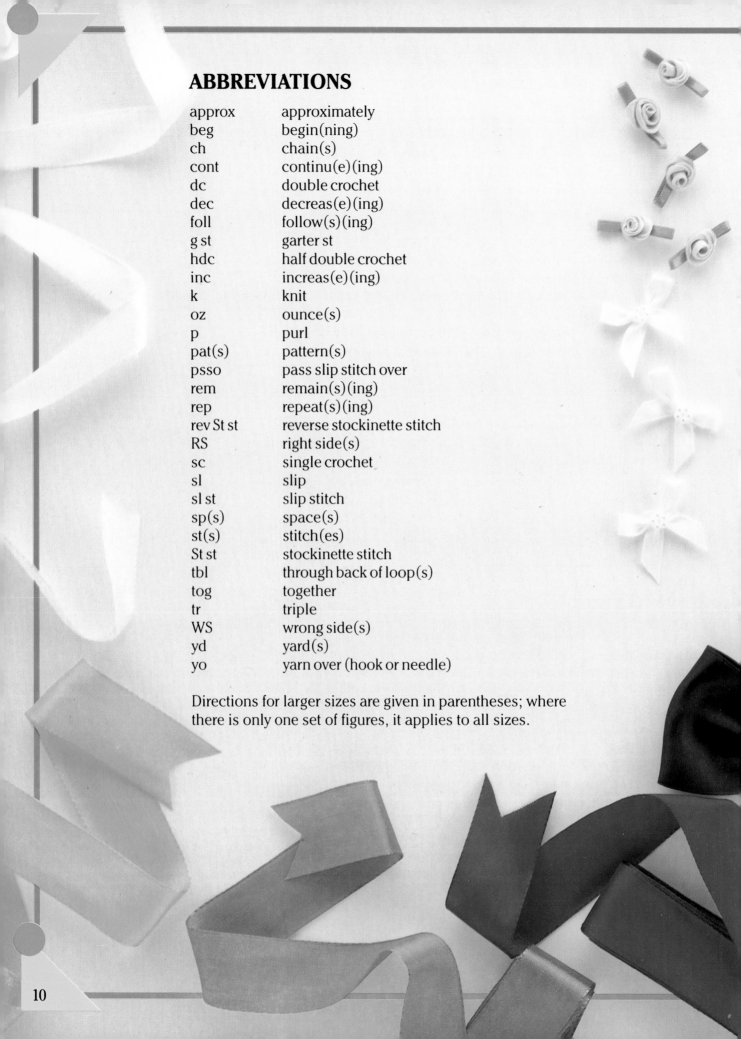

ABBREVIATIONS

approx	approximately
beg	begin(ning)
ch	chain(s)
cont	continu(e)(ing)
dc	double crochet
dec	decreas(e)(ing)
foll	follow(s)(ing)
g st	garter st
hdc	half double crochet
inc	increas(e)(ing)
k	knit
oz	ounce(s)
p	purl
pat(s)	pattern(s)
psso	pass slip stitch over
rem	remain(s)(ing)
rep	repeat(s)(ing)
rev St st	reverse stockinette stitch
RS	right side(s)
sc	single crochet
sl	slip
sl st	slip stitch
sp(s)	space(s)
st(s)	stitch(es)
St st	stockinette stitch
tbl	through back of loop(s)
tog	together
tr	triple
WS	wrong side(s)
yd	yard(s)
yo	yarn over (hook or needle)

Directions for larger sizes are given in parentheses; where there is only one set of figures, it applies to all sizes.

INDIVIDUAL STYLE

Much of the fun of knitting your own clothes comes from adding your own personal touches. You can start by deciding the colors you want to work with. It may be that your son or daughter needs a sweater to team with a particular pair of pants or a skirt, so do not feel restricted by the colors selected in this book.

Browsing through the shelves of a yarn shop, you will find that the color choice of ordinary sport yarns is vast. If your local shop only stocks a few colors, they may have a selection of color cards for you to choose from and will then order a yarn specially for you. Always buy enough yarn, whether your yarn has to be specially ordered or is currently in stock, as it is important to knit your garment from the same dye lot.

A selection of buttons, ribbons, and collars have also been used in this book. Children's buttons can be enchanting and there is such a vast range currently available. You might like to sew your child's name to the front of a jacket using lettered buttons, or use specially shaped buttons depicting stars, hearts, bows, fruit, airplanes, or boats. Our accessories and trimmings are simply suggestions. You may, for instance, prefer to trim your baby blanket with felt flowers instead of embroidered ones or thread strips of narrow lace or ricric braiding through a sweater instead of ribbon.

In addition to providing a whole wardrobe of designs for your young family, the aim of this book is to inspire knitters to show just how versatile the results can be when working with a few balls of yarn and a pair of knitting needles.

Basic Knitting Techniques

Binding on

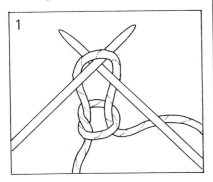

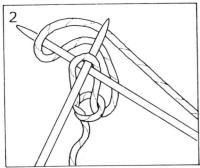

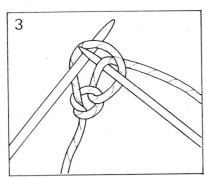

CASTING ON

Make a slip knot on your left-hand needle, making sure that it is not too tight. Now, insert the point of your right-hand needle into the loop (1). Take the yarn and bring it first under and then over your right-hand needle (2). Bring the yarn through the slip knot to make a new loop (3). Place the new loop on your left-hand needle. Insert your right-hand needle between the two loops wrapping the yarn under and then over the tip of the right-hand needle (4). Bring the right-hand needle with the yarn around it back to the front between the two loops (5). Place the new loop on the left-hand needle and continue in this way until you have the necessary number of stitches (6).

BINDING OFF

Knit two stitches rather loosely. Then, using the tip of your left-hand needle, lift the first stitch over the second and off the needle. Continue binding off in this way.

KNITTING

Take your right-hand needle and, with your yarn at the back of the work, insert it through the first stitch on your left-hand needle (1). Wrap the yarn around the tip of your needle (2). Draw a loop through and then slip the old stitch off your left-hand needle, keeping the new stitch on the right-hand one (3).

PURLING

With the yarn at the front of your work, insert the right-hand needle through the first stitch on the left-hand needle in front of the left-hand needle (1). Wrap the yarn around the tip of your

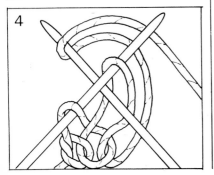

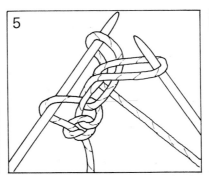

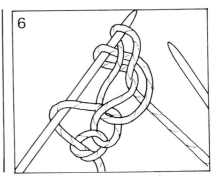

right-hand needle (2). Draw a loop through and working on the same principle as the knit stitch, discard the old stitch on the left-hand needle while retaining the new one on the right (3).

The three most common types of knitting are garter stitch, stockinette stitch, and ribbing. Ribbing is most often used on the cuffs and lower edges of garments to create a slightly tighter finish so that the garment retains its shape. It is usually worked on smaller needles than the rest of the garment. Ribbing is achieved by working either one or two knit stitches and then one or two purl stitches alternately along the row. Garter stitch is ideal for beginners and it is simply knitting every row. Stockinette stitch is the most widely used type of stitch and is formed by knitting one row and then purling the next and so on.

INCREASING
Knit or purl into your stitch but do not discard the stitch on the left-hand needle. Instead, knit or purl into the back of it, thus creating two stitches from one.

DECREASING
Insert your right-hand needle into the next stitch in the usual way but this time through two stitches instead of one. Work the two stitches as one thereby decreasing one stitch. This principle applies to both knit and purl rows.

Binding off

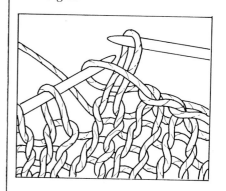

Knitting

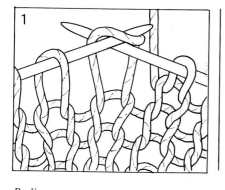

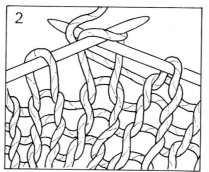

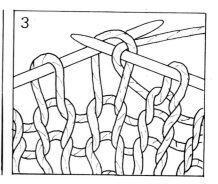

Purling

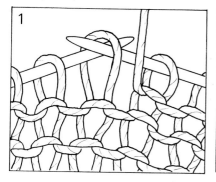

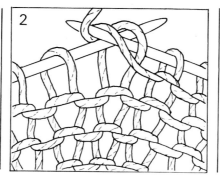

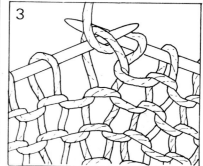

Basic Crochet Techniques

FOUNDATION CHAIN

Crochet is built around the chain stitch. It is made by a series of loops, each one being drawn through the preceding one until you have the required number. Make a slip knot on your hook holding it in your right hand with the yarn in your left hand, and manoeuvre the hook so that it goes first under and then over the yarn (1), thus creating the loop (2) which is then drawn through the original loop for form a chain (3).

SINGLE CROCHET

Having created your basic chain row, take the hook and insert it into the second chain from the hook. Wrap the yarn over the hook and draw a loop through (1), then wrap the yarn over again (2) and draw the yarn through both loops (3).

DOUBLE CROCHET

With your basic chain row, wrap the yarn over the hook and then insert it into the fifth chain. Wrap the yarn over the hook and draw a loop through (1). Then wrap the yarn over the hook and draw it through the first two loops on the hook (2). Wrap the yarn over the hook again and draw it through two loops thus creating a double crochet (3).

SLIP STITCH

Insert the hook into the second chain from the hook. Wrap the yarn over the hook (1) and pull it through the chain stitch and the loop on the hook, leaving one loop on hook (2).

Foundation chain

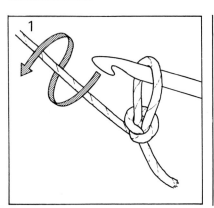
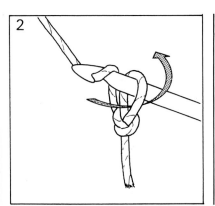
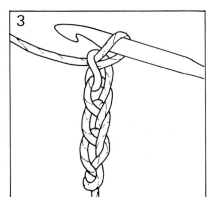

Single crochet

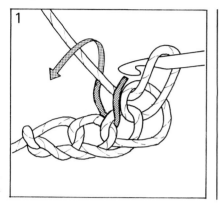

1

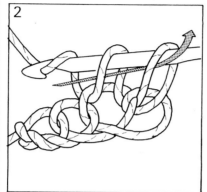

2

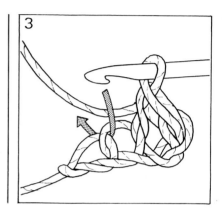

3

Double crochet

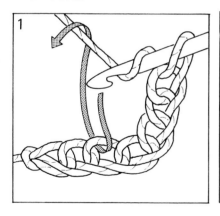

1

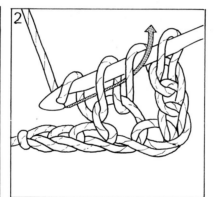

2

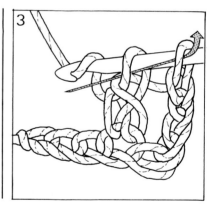

3

Slip stitch

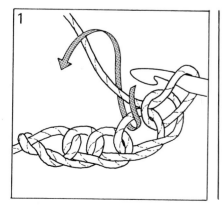

1

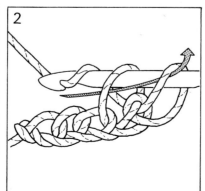

2

Ring–a–ring o'roses

Ring–a–ring o'roses,
A pocket full of posies,
A–tishoo, a–tishoo!
We all fall down.

Baby Coat, Dress, and Blanket Cover

Baby Coat, Dress, and Blanket

MATERIALS
Wendy *Family Choice DK* or other sport yarn for coat and dress:
10½oz in White (A)
Wendy *Family Choice Chunky* or other bulky weight yarn for blanket:
5¼oz in White (B)
2yd of ready-made embroidered flowers or other trimming and matching thread
2 buttons
One pair each of sizes 3, 5, 6, and 10½ needles *or size to obtain correct gauge*
Size D crochet hook

MEASUREMENTS
To fit approx 6-12 months
Finished coat chest measurement 25½"
Coat length 12"
Blanket 16½" by 21¾"

GAUGE
22 sts and 30 rows to 4" over St st using size 6 needles and A
To save time, take time to check gauge.

ABBREVIATIONS
See page 10 for abbreviations.

COAT

BODY
Using size 5 needles and A, cast on 40 sts for Right Front and work 1" in g st. Work in St st until Front measures 6¾" from beg, ending with a RS row. Inc one st at beg of next row, work one row even, inc one st at beg of next row.
Work one row even, then at beg of every other row cast on 2 sts 4 times, then 13 sts once. 63 sts.
Cont in St st until Front measures 11" from beg, ending with a WS row.

Neck Shaping
Bind off 5 sts at beg of next row and then at beg of every other row 2 sts twice and one st twice. 52 sts.
Work even until Front measures 12¼" from beg, ending with a WS row. Leave sts on a spare needle.

Left Front
Work as for Right Front, reversing shaping.

Next row K52 sts, cast on 16 sts and k52 sts from spare needle. 120 sts.

Back
Work even until piece measures 15¾" from beg, ending with a WS row.
Bind off 13 sts at beg of next 2 rows, then 2 sts at beg of next 8 rows and one st at beg of next 4 rows. 74 sts.
Work even until piece measures 23½", ending with a WS row.
Work 1" in g st and bind off.
Pick up and k32 sts along sleeve edges and work 1" in g st. Bind off.

HOOD
Using size 5 needles and A, cast on 76 sts. Work in St st until Hood measures 4¾" from beg, ending with a WS row. To shape head bind off 2 sts at beg of next 6 rows.

Back Shaping
1st row Bind off 2 sts, k30 sts, turn leaving rem sts on spare needle.
2nd row Purl.
3rd row Bind off 2 sts, k to end.
4th row Bind off 3 sts, p to end.
5th-8th rows Rep 3rd and 4th rows twice.
9th row Bind off 3 sts, k to end.
10th row As 4th row.
11the row As 9th row.
12th row Bind off 3 sts, p to end. Bind off rem 3 sts.
Rejoin yarn to center of Hood and complete other side of Hood to match, reversing shaping.
Pick up and k74 sts around front edge of Hood, work 1" in g st and bind off.

FINISHING
Join side and sleeve seams. Join back hood seam and sew base of Hood to neck edge. Sew trimming up Right Front along edge, around edge of Hood and down Left Front, using matching thread.

DRESS

BACK
**Using size 5 needles and A, cast on 132 sts and work in k1, p1 rib for ¾", ending with a WS row.

Change to size 6 needles and work in St st until Back measures 8" from beg, ending with a RS row.
Next row [P2tog] 18 times, [p3tog] 20 times, [p2tog] 18 times. 56 sts.
Change to size 5 needles and work in k1, p1 rib for ¾", ending with a WS row.

Armhole Shaping
Bind off 4 sts at beg of next 2 rows and 2 sts at beg of foll 2 rows. 44 sts.
Dec one st at each end of next and then every other row until 40 sts rem, ending with a WS row.**
Next row (RS) K18 sts and slip these sts onto a spare needle, bind off 4 sts, k to end.
Cont in St st on these sts only, until Back measures 11½" from beg, ending with a WS row.

Neck Shaping
Bind off 4 sts at beg of next row, work one row even and bind off 3 sts at beg of next row. 11 sts.
Work even until Back measures 12" from beg. Bind off.
Rejoin yarn to neck edge of rem sts and complete to match first side, reversing shaping.

FRONT
Work as for Back from ** to **.
Work even in St st on rem 40 sts until Front measures 10½" from beg, ending with a WS row.

Neck Shaping
Next row K16 sts and slip these sts onto a spare needle, bind off 8 sts, k to end.
Cont in St st on these sts only, work one row even. *Bind off 2 sts at beg of next row and work one row even *, then rep from * to * once. Dec one st at neck edge on next row. Work even on rem 11 sts until Front matches Back to shoulder. Bind off.
Rejoin yarn to neck edge of sts on spare needle and complete to match first side, reversing shaping.

SLEEVES
Using size 3 needles and A, cast on 32 sts and work in k1, p1 rib for ¾", inc 8 sts evenly across last (WS) row.
40 sts.

Change to size 6 needles and work in St st until Sleeve measures 2½" from beg, ending with a WS row.

Cap Shaping
Bind off 3 sts at beg of next 2 rows and 2 sts at beg of foll 2 rows. 30 sts. Dec one st at each end of next and every foll 5th row until 24 sts rem, ending with a WS row. Bind off 2 sts at beg of next 2 rows and 3 sts at beg of foll 2 rows. Bind off rem 14 sts. Make 2nd Sleeve in same way.

BUTTONHOLE BAND
With RS facing and using size 3 needles and A, pick up and k12 sts along right back opening. Work ½" in k1, p1 rib, ending with a WS row.
Next row (RS) Rib 2 sts, bind off 2 sts, rib 3, bind off 2 sts, rib to end.
Next row (WS) Work in rib, casting on 2 sts over those bound off. Cont in rib until Band measures ¾". Bind off in rib.

BUTTON BAND
Work as for Buttonhole Band on left back opening, omitting buttonholes.

FINISHING
Join shoulder seams. Sew Sleeves to armholes, gathering sleeve cap. Join side and sleeve seams. Sew lower ends of back bands to bound off sts.
With RS facing and using crochet hook and A, work one row of sc evenly around neck edge, join with sl st to first sc, turn and work 1 sc in each sc to end, join with a sl st. Fasten off. Sew on buttons. Sew separate motifs of trimming onto back and front yokes.

BLANKET

TO MAKE
Using size 10½ needles and B, cast on 56 sts. Work 4 rows in g st.
1st pat row (WS) K2, p52, k2.
2nd pat row K.
Cont rep first and 2nd pat rows until Blanket measures 21½" from beg, ending with a RS row. Work 3 rows in g st and bind off knitwise. Using matching thread, sew trimming to RS of short ends of Blanket below g st.

Mary Had a Little Lamb

Mary had a little lamb,
Its fleece was white as snow,
And everywhere that Mary went
The lamb was sure to go.

Cardigan with Hood, Leggings, Mittens, and Toy Lamb

Cardigan with Hood, Leggings, Mittens, and Toy Lamb

MATERIALS

Wendy *Peter Pan Darling 4 ply* or other sport yarn for cardigan and mittens:

9 (12)oz in Pink or Blue (A)

1½oz in White (B)

Wendy *DK* or other knitting worsted yarn for toy lamb:

3oz in White (C)

7 buttons

2 toy eyes

Stuffing for toy

Black embroidery thread

One pair each of sizes 2, 3, and 6 needles *or size to obtain correct gauge*

MEASUREMENTS

To fit approx 6 (12) months

Finished chest measurement 21 (22½)″

Cardigan length 10½ (12¾)″

Sleeve seam 6¾ (8½)″

Inside leg seam 9 (9½)″

GAUGE

14 sts and 18 rows to 2″ over St st using size 3 needles

To save time, take time to check gauge.

ABBREVIATIONS

See page 10 for abbreviations.

CARDIGAN

BACK

Using size 2 needles and A, cast on 73 (79) sts.

1st row (RS) K1, *p1, k1, rep from * to end.

2nd row P1, *k1, p1, rep from * to end.

Rep these 2 rows for 1½″.

Change to size 3 needles and cont in St st until Back measures 10½ (12¾)″ from beg, ending with a p row.

Shoulder Shaping

Bind off 26 (28) sts at beg of next 2 rows. Bind off rem 21 (23) sts.

LEFT FRONT

Using size 2 needles and A, cast on 34 (36) sts.

1st row (RS) *K1, p1, rep from * to last 2 sts, k2.

2nd row P2, * k1, p1, rep from * to end.

Rep these 2 rows for 1½″.

Change to size 3 needles and cont in St st until Front measures 8½ (10½)″ from beg, ending with a k row.

Shaping Neck

Bind off 3 sts at beg of next row. Then dec one st at neck edge on next 3 rows, then on every other row 2 (3) times. 26 (28) sts.

Work even until Front measures same as Back to shoulder, ending with a p row. Bind off.

RIGHT FRONT

Using size 2 needles and A, cast on 34 (36) sts.

1st row (RS) K2, *p1, k1 rep from * to end.

2nd row *P1, k1, rep from * to last 2 sts, p2.

Rep these 2 rows for 1½″.

Change to size 3 needles and cont in St st until Front measures 5½ (6)″ from beg, ending with a p row.

Place lamb motif as foll:

Next row K10 (11)A, 2B, 11A, 2B, 9 (10)A.

Cont in St st foll chart from 2nd row until all 20 chart rows have been completed.

Then using A only, cont in St st until Right Front measures same as Left Front to neck shaping, ending with a p row. Shape neck as for Left Front, work one row less to shoulder and bind off on WS.

SLEEVES

Using size 2 needles and B, cast on 41 (45) sts and work in rib as for Back for 1½″, ending with a RS row.

Next row Rib 4 (2), *work into front and back of next st — called inc —, rib 3, rep from * to last 5 (3) sts, inc in next st, rib to end. 50 (56) sts.

Change to size 3 needles and A and work 10 rows in St st.

Inc one st at each end of next and every foll 6th (8)th row until there are 62 (68) sts.

Work even until Sleeve measures 6¾ (8½)″ from beg, ending with a k row. Bind off.

Make 2nd Sleeve in same way.

BUTTON BAND

Using size 2 needles and A and with RS facing, pick up and k69 (87) sts evenly along Left Front edge of Girl's Jacket or Right Front edge of Boy's Jacket.

Work 8 rows in rib as for Back, beg with a WS row. Bind off in rib.

BUTTONHOLE BAND

Using size 2 needles and A and with RS facing, pick up and k69 (87) sts evenly along Right Front edge of Girl's Jacket or Left Front edge of Boy's Jacket. Work 3 rows in rib as for Back, beg with a WS row.

Next row Rib 3 (4), bind off 2 sts, *rib until there are 13 (17) sts on right-hand needle after binding off, bind off 2 sts, rep from * 3 times more, rib to end.

Next row Work in rib, casting on 2 sts over those bound off in last row. Work 3 rows in rib. Bind off in rib. Join shoulder seams. Sew Sleeves to armhole, matching center to shoulder seam. Join sleeve and side seams and sew on buttons.

HOOD

Using size 2 needles and B, cast on 127 (143) sts and work 8 rows in rib as for Back.

Change to size 3 needles and A and beg with a k row, work 8 rows in St st.

Next row K1, k2tog tbl, k to last 3 sts, k2tog, k1.

Next row K1, p2tog, p to last 3 sts, p2tog tbl, k1.

Rep these last 2 rows 3 (4) times more. 111 (123) sts.

Work even for 10 (8) rows in St st, so ending with a p row.

Center Shaping

1st row K53 (59) sts, k2tog, k1, k2tog tbl, k53 (59) sts.

2nd and foll WS rows K1, p to last st, k1.

3rd row K52 (58) sts, k2tog, k1, k2tog tbl, k52 (58) sts.

Cont to dec one st at each side of center st as before, working one st less in St st each time until there are 95 (105) sts, ending with a p row.

Next row Bind off 4 sts, k41 (46) sts including st already on needle after

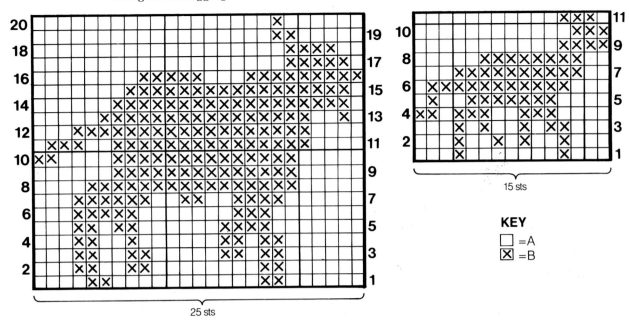

Cardigan and leggings motif — 25 sts

Mitten motif — 15 sts

KEY
☐ = A
☒ = B

bind off, k2tog, k1, k2tog tbl, k to end.
Next row Bind off 4 sts, p40 (45), p2tog tbl, p1, p2tog, p to last st, k1.
Cont to bind off 4 sts at beg of every row and dec one st at each side of center st as for last 2 rows until there are 47 (45) sts, ending with a p row. Bind off.

FINISHING
Join back seam of Hood. Sew Hood to neck edge of Cardigan beg and ending halfway across front bands.

LEGGINGS

LEGS
Using size 2 needles and A, cast on 25 (27) sts. Work in rib for 1½" as for Back, ending with a RS row.
Next row P1 (2), *(inc in next st) twice, p1, rep from * to last 3 (4) sts, inc in next st, p2 (3) sts. 40 (42) sts.
Change to size 3 needles and work in St st until Leg measures 9 (9½)" from beg, ending with a p row.
Leave sts on a st holder.
Make 3 more Legs in same way.

BACK
** With RS facing and using A, k across 40 (42) sts of one Leg, turn and cast on 7 (9) sts. Turn work

again and k across 40 (42) sts of another leg. 87 (93) sts.
Work 3 rows in St st, so ending with a p row. Dec one st at each end of next and every foll 4th row until 75 (79) sts rem.**
Work even until Back measures 6¼ (6½)" from crotch cast-on sts, ending with a p row.

Back Shaping
Next 2 rows Work to last 6 sts, turn.
Next 2 rows Work to last 12 sts, turn.
Next 2 rows Work to last 18 sts, turn.
Next 2 rows Work to last 24 sts, turn.
Next 2 rows Work to last 30 sts, turn.
Next row K to end.
Next row P.
Change to size 2 needles and work in k1, p1 rib for 1½".
Bind off in rib.

FRONT
Work as for Back from ** to **.
P one row.
Place lamb motif as foll:
Next row K14A, 2B, 11A, 2B, 46 (50)A.
Cont in St st foll chart from 2nd row until all 20 chart rows have been completed.

Then using A only, cont in St st until side measures same as Back from cast-on edge to ribbing.
Change to size 2 needles and work in k1, p1 rib for 1½", ending with a WS row. Change to size 3 needles.
Next row Bind off 16 sts in rib, rib 9, k25 (29) sts, rib to end.
Next row Bind off 16 sts in rib, rib 9, p25 (29) sts, rib 9.
Next row Rib 9, k25 (29) sts, rib 9.
Next row Rib 9, p25 (29) sts, rib 9.
Rep these last 2 rows 12 (14) times more.
Change to size 2 needles and work 4 rows in rib.
Next row (buttonhole row) Rib 4, bind off 2 sts, rib 31 (35), bind off 2 sts, rib to end.
Next row Work in rib, casting on 2 sts over those bound off in last row.
Work 3 rows in rib. Bind off in rib.

STRAPS
Using size 2 needles and A, cast on 9 sts. Work in k1, p1 rib until Strap measures 14 (15)" from beg.
Bind off in rib.
Make 2nd Strap in same way.

FINISHING
Join side and leg seams.
Sew straps at back of waist and sew one button to end of each strap

23

to fit buttonhole on bib.

MITTENS

LEFT-HAND MITTEN

*** Using size 2 needles and A, cast on 37 (39) sts.
Work in k1, p1 rib for 12 rows, inc one st at end of last row. 38 (40) sts.
Change to size 3 needles and beg with a k row, work 4 rows in St st.***
Place lamb motif as foll:
Next row K6A, 1B, 7A, 1B, 23 (25)A.
Cont in St st foll chart from 2nd row until all 11 chart rows have been completed.

Work 5 (7) rows more in St st.

Top Shaping
1st row K1, *k2tog tbl, k14 (15), k2tog, rep from * once more, k1.
2nd and foll WS rows P.
3rd row K1, *k2tog tbl, k12 (13), k2tog, rep from * once more, k1.
5th row K1, *k2tog tbl, k10 (11), k2tog, rep from * once more, k1.
7th row K1, *k2tog tbl, k8 (9), k2tog, rep from * once more, k1.
Bind off.

RIGHT-HAND MITTEN

Work as for Left-hand Mitten, but reversing motif by working first chart row from right to left as a p row.

FINISHING

Join top and side seams.

TOY LAMB

BODY AND SIDES OF HEAD

Using size 6 needles and C, cast on 29 sts.
1st row K.
2nd row Inc 1 in first st, k to last 2 sts, inc in next st — called inc 1 —, k1.
Knit 3 rows.
6th row Inc 1, k to end.
Knit 3 rows.
10th row As 2nd row.
Knit 3 rows.
14th row As 6th row.

Knit 5 rows.
20th row K to last 3 sts, k2tog, k1.
Knit 3 rows.
Work the last 4 rows once more and then the 20th row again.
Knit one row. 32 sts.

Divide for Side of Head
1st row (RS) K1, k2tog, k6, k2tog, k1, turn leaving rem 20 sts on a st holder.
2nd row K.
3rd row K to last 3 sts, k2tog, k1.
4th-12th rows K.
13th row Inc 1, k to end.
14th row K to last 2 sts, inc 1, k1.
15th row As 13th row.
16th row K.
17th row Cast on 4 sts, k to end.
18th-24th rows K.
25th row Bind off 5 sts, k to end.
26th row K.
27th row Bind off 2 sts, k to end.
28th-30th rows K.
31st row Bind off 3 sts, k to last 3 sts, k2tog, k1.
32nd row K1, k2tog, k to end.
Bind off.
With RS facing, rejoin C at head end to 20 sts on st holder and knit 4 rows.
Next row K to last 3 sts, k2tog, k1.
Next row K.
Next row K to last 2 sts, inc 1, k1.
Knit 3 rows.
Leave these 20 sts on a st holder to use later.

Second Side of Head
Using size 6 needles and C, cast on 4 sts.
1st row K.
2nd row Inc 1, k to end.
3rd row Cast on 3 sts, k to last 2 sts, inc 1, k1. 9 sts.
4th-6th rows K.
7th row Cast on 2 sts, k to end.
8th row K.
9th row Cast on 5 sts, k to end. 16 sts.
10th-16th rows K.
17th row Bind off 4 sts, k to end. 12 sts.
18th row K.
19th-21st rows K1, k2tog, k to end.
22nd-30th rows K. 9sts.
31st row K to last 2 sts, inc 1, k1.
32nd row K.
33rd row Inc 1, k to last 2 sts, inc 1, k1, then knit across the 20 sts on

the st holder.
34th row K.
35th row K to last 2 sts, inc 1, k1.
36th-38th row K.
Rep last 4 rows twice more. 35 sts.
47th and 48th rows K.
49th row K1, k2tog, k to end.
50th-52nd rows K.
53rd row K1, k2tog, k to last 3 sts, k2tog, k1.
54th-56th rows K.
57th row K1, k2tog, k to end.
58th-60th rows K.
61st row K1, k2tog, k to last 3 sts, k2tog, k1.
Bind off.

HEAD GUSSET
Using size 6 needles and C, cast on 3 sts.
1st row Inc 2, k1.
2nd-6th rows K.
7th row Inc 1, k to last 2 sts, inc 1, k1.
8th-12th rows K.
13th-24th rows Rep 7th-12th rows twice more.
25th row As 7th row. 13 sts.
26th row K.
Rep last 2 rows 5 times more. 23 sts.
37th-45th rows K.

Back of Head Shaping
46th row K1, k2tog, k to last 3 sts, k2tog, k1. 21 sts.
47th-49th rows K.
50th row K1, k2tog, k2, k2tog, k7, k2tog, k2, k2tog, k1. 17 sts.
51st-53rd rows K.
54th row K1, k2tog, k2, k2tog, k3, k2tog, k2, k2tog, k1. 13 sts.
55th-57th rows K.
58th row K1, k2tog, k7, k2tog, k1.
Knit 8 rows. Bind off rem 11 sts.

EARS
Using size 6 needles and C, cast on 3 sts.
1st row Inc 2, k1.
2nd row Inc 1, k2, inc 1, k1.
3rd and 4th rows K.
5th row Inc 1, k to last 2 sts, inc 1, k1.
6th-26th rows K.
27th row K.
28th row K1, p to last st, k1.
Rep last 2 rows 5 times more.
39th row K1, k2tog, k to last 3 sts, k2tog, k1.
40th row As 28th row.

Rep last 2 rows once more.
43rd row K1, sl 1, k2tog, psso, k1.
Bind off.
Fold Ear in half and overcast around open edge.
Make 2nd Ear in same way.

LEGS
Using size 6 needles and C, cast on 18 sts and knit 24 rows.
Dec row K1, k2tog, k to last 3 sts, k2tog, k1.
Knit 15 rows.
*Work dec row once more and knit 5 rows, rep from *once more.
Next row K2tog to end. 6 sts.
Break off yarn, thread long loose end through rem sts and pull tightly, fold Leg in half and sew side seam.
Make 3 more Legs in same way.

TAIL
Using size 6 needles and C, cast on 13 sts and knit 18 rows.
Dec row K1, k2tog, k to last 3 sts, k2tog, k1.
Knit 5 rows.
Work dec row once more and then knit 3 rows.
Work dec row once more. 7 sts.
Break off yarn and complete as for Legs.

COLLAR
Using size 2 needles and B, cast on 5 sts.
Work in k1, p1 rib until Collar is long enough to fit around lamb's neck plus an extra 1½″ for overlap.
Next row K1, sl 1, k2tog, psso, k1.
Next row P3tog.
Fasten off.

FINISHING
Join bound-off edge of gusset to center back neck. Sew up each side of back neck over top of head to end of muzzle, with widest part of gusset at top of head. Sew tog nose edges and join seam down center front.
Join back seam, leaving lower edge open.
Insert eyes and stuff head and body and join rem seam. Stuff legs and attach to body. Stuff tail loosely and attach to body. Sew on ears and embroider nose and mouth.
Position collar and join seam.

Bye, Baby Bunting

Bye, Baby Bunting,
Father's gone a hunting
Gone to get a rabbit skin,
To wrap the baby bunting in.

Sweater, Pants, and Cap

MATERIALS
Emu *Superwash DK* or other sport yarn:
8¾oz in Cream (A)
1¾oz each in Blue (B), Green (C), Gray (D), and Yellow (E)
3 buttons
Elastic thread for trousers
One pair each of sizes 3 and 6

needles *or size to obtain correct gauge*
Size E crochet hook

MEASUREMENTS
To fit approx 6-12 months
Finished chest measurement 18½″
Sweater length 11¾″
Sleeve seam 8½″
Inside leg seam 9½″

GAUGE
20 sts and 40 rows to 4″ over g st using size 6 needles
To save time, take time to check gauge.

ABBREVIATIONS
See page 10 for abbreviations.

SWEATER

FRONT
Using size 3 needles and A, cast on 46 sts.
1st rib row K3, [p2, k2] to last st, k1.
2nd rib row K1, [p2, k2] to last 3 sts, p2, k1.
Rep last 2 rows until 14 rows have been worked from beg.
Change to size 6 needles and work in g st in stripe pat as foll:
2 rows in B, 2 rows in C, 2 rows in D, 2 rows in E, and 2 rows in A.
Rep last 10 rows until Front measures 10″ from beg.

Neck Shaping
Next row K19, turn leaving rem sts on a spare needle.
Cont in pat dec one st at neck edge on next 4 rows. 15 sts.
Work even for 11 rows. Bind off.
Rejoin yarn to RS off rem sts, bind off center 8 sts and complete to match first side, reversing shaping.

BACK
Work as for Front until Back measures same as Front to shoulder, omitting neck shaping.
Next row Bind off 30 sts loosely, k to end.
Next row Bind off 4 sts, k to end. Work 6 rows on rem sts for button band and bind off.

SLEEVES
Using size 3 needles and A, cast on

28 sts.
Work 12 rows in rib as for Front, inc 4 sts evenly across last row.
Change to size 6 needles and working in g st and stripe pat as set, work 10 rows. Inc one st at each end of next row and then on every foll 8th row until there are 40 sts.
Work even until Sleeve measures 8½″ from beg. Bind off.
Make 2nd Sleeve in same way.

NECKBAND
Join right shoulder seam.
Using size 3 needles and A, pick up and k10 sts down left front neck, 10 sts across center front neck, 10 sts up right front neck, 18 sts across back neck and 4 sts across button band. 52 sts.
Work 5 rows in rib as for Front and bind off loosely in rib.

FINISHING
Sew tog 7 sts on outside of left shoulder. Sew Sleeves to Back and Front. Join side and sleeve seams. Crochet 3 buttonhole loops on front left shoulder and sew on buttons.

TROUSERS

FRONT
* Using size 6 needles and A, cast on 20 sts. Work in g st for 8″, then slip sts of first leg onto a spare needle.
Work 2nd leg in the same way.
Next row K to end, cast on 8 sts for crotch and k across sts on spare needle. 48 sts.
Cont working in g st until Front measures 6½″ from crotch, ending with a WS row.*
** Change to size 3 needles and work 6 rows in rib as for Sweater. Bind off in rib.**

BACK
Work as for Front from * to *. 48 sts.
Next row K to last 3 sts, turn.
Next row Sl 1, k to last 3 sts, turn.
Next 2 rows Sl 1, k to last 6 sts, turn.
Next 2 rows Sl 1, k to last 9 sts, turn.
Next 2 rows Sl 1, k to last 12 sts, turn.
Next 2 rows Sl 1, k to last 15 sts, turn.
Next row Sl 1, k to last 16 sts, turn.

Next row Sl 1, k to end, dec 2 sts evenly across row. Complete as for Front from ** to **.

FINISHING
Join side seams.
Thread elastic in and out of top 3 rows of ribbing at waist.

CAP

TO MAKE
Using size 6 needles and A, cast on 81 sts. Work 20 rows in g st in stripe pat as set for sweater.
Then cont in A only.
Next row K.
Next row K1, p to last st, k1.
Rep last 2 rows 4 times more.
Beg shaping as foll:
1st row *K9, k into front and back of next st — called inc 1 —, rep from * to last st, k1.
2nd and foll WS rows K1, p to last st, K1.
3rd row *K10, inc 1, rep from * to last st, k1.
5th row *K11, inc 1, rep from * to last st, k1.
7th row *K12, inc 1, rep from * to last st, k1.
Cont in this way working one more st between incs on RS rows until there are 137 sts.
Work even for 1″, ending with a WS row. Then dec as foll:
1st row K1,*k15, k2tog, rep from * to end of row.
2nd and foll WS rows K1, p to last st, k1.
3rd row K1,*k14, k2tog, rep from * to end of row.
5th row K1,*k13, k2tog, rep from * to end of row.
7th row K1,*k12, k2tog, rep from * to end of row.
Cont in this way working one st less between decs on RS rows until 17 sts rem, ending with a WS row.
Next row K1, * k2tog, rep from * to end of row.
Break off yarn, thread through rem sts and pull tightly.

FINISHING
Join seam. Using crochet hook and A, make a 6″ length of chain and fasten to top of cap. Attach tassel to end of chain, using 8″ strands of A, B, C, D, and E folded in half.

RABBIT

MATERIALS

Emu *DK* or any other sport yarn:
1¾oz in Brown (A)
Small amount in White (B), Black
(C), and Blue (D)
Stuffing
One pair of size 6 needles

MEASUREMENT

Height approx 9″

BODY

Using size 6 needles and A, cast on
38 sts and k 38 rows. Bind off
tightly. Fold Body in half lengthwise
and join side seam.
For base of rabbit, using size 6
needles and A, cast on 4 sts.
1st row K.
2nd row K, inc one st at each end
of row.
Rep last 2 rows twice more, then k 3
rows more.
10th row K, dec one st at each end
of row.
11th row K.
Rep last 2 rows twice more. Bind
off. Join base to one end of body.
Stuff body. Gather rem open end,
leaving opening 1¼″ in diameter.

HEAD

Using size 6 needles and A, cast on
14 sts and k 4 rows.
1st row K into front and back of
first st — called inc 1 —, k to end.
2nd row K to last st, inc 1.
3rd row Inc 1, k to last st, inc 1.
4th row K.
5th and 6th rows As first and 2nd
rows.
7th-10th rows K.
Mark end of last row with a
coloured thread to indicate
position of nose.
11th row K2tog, k to end.
12th row K to last 2 sts, k2tog.
13th row As 11th row.
14th row K.
Rep last 2 rows 3 times more.
Dec one st at each end of next row,
then k one row. Rep last 2 rows
twice more. Bind off.
Make 2nd piece in same way.

HEAD GUSSET

Using size 6 needles and A, cast on
3 sts.

Working in g st throughout, work 3
rows, then inc one st at each end of
next row. Rep last 4 rows 8 times
more. Work 4 rows.
Dec one st at each end of next row,
then work 3 rows. Rep last 4 rows 5
times more. Bind off.
Sew gusset between head pieces,
beg at nose. Join rem seam, leaving
neck open. Stuff head firmly.
Gather neck opening. Embroider
eyes, nose, mouth, and whiskers
using C, and center of eyes using D.

EARS

Using size 6 needles and A, cast on
6 sts.
Working in g st throughout, work 2
rows, then inc one st at each end of
next row. Rep last 3 rows 7 times
more. Knit 9 rows. Bind off.
Make 3 more pieces in same way.
Sew pieces tog in pairs leaving
bound-off edges open. Turn right
side out and join bound-off edges.
Fold lower edge of ears in half and
join to head.

LEGS

Using size 6 needles and A, cast on
22 sts and k 10 rows. Bind off.

Make 3 more pieces in same way.
To make pad, using A, cast on 4 sts.
Working in g st throughout, work
one row, then inc one st at each end
of next row. Rep last 2 rows once
more. Work even for 2 rows.
Dec one st at each end of next row,
then work even for one row. Rep
last 2 rows once more. Bind off.
Make 3 more pieces in same way.
Fold each leg in half and join sides.
Join a pad to one end of each leg.
Turn right side out and stuff. Then
join openings and sew each leg to
body.

TAIL

Using size 6 needles and B, cast on
7 sts.
Working in g st throughout, work 2
rows, then inc one st at each end of
next row. Rep last 3 rows 3 times
more. Work even for 3 rows.
Dec one st at each end of next row,
then work even for 2 rows. Rep last
3 rows twice more.
Dec one st at each end of next row.
Bind off.
Make 2nd piece in same way.
Sew pieces tog leaving an opening.
Turn right side out and stuff firmly.
Join opening and sew tail to body.

Oranges and Lemons

Oranges and Lemons,
Say the bells of St Clement's.
You owe me five farthings
Say the bells of St Martin's.

MATERIALS
Twilleys *Stalite* or other lightweight cotton yarn:
Sweater
3½ (5¼, 8¾)oz in White (A),
1¾oz each in Yellow (B) and Orange (C)
Short Pants
1¾oz (3½, 3½)oz in White (A)
Bib
1¾oz in White (A)
3 buttons for sweater
Waist length of ½" wide elastic for pants
20" of narrow ribbon for bib
One pair each of sizes 2 and 3 needles *or size to obtain correct gauge*
Size B crochet hook

MEASUREMENTS
To fit approx 6 (12, 18) months
Finished chest measurement 19¼ (21¼, 23½)"
Sweater length 10 (11, 13)"
Sleeve seam 3½ (4¼, 5)"

GAUGE
30 sts and 36 rows to 4" over pat using size 3 needles
To save time, take time to check gauge.

ABBREVIATIONS
See page 10 for abbreviations.

Baby's
Two-piece Outfit and Bib

SWEATER

BACK

** Using size 2 needles and A, cast on 60 (68, 76) sts. Work in k1, p1 rib for 1", inc 12 sts evenly across last row. 72 (80, 88) sts.

Change to size 3 needles and work in stripe pat as foll:

Beg with a k row, work in St st, working 2 rows B, 2 rows C and 2 rows A, so ending with a WS row. Work in pat from motif chart, working different colors by loosely stranding yarn at back of work over no more than 3 sts at a time, reading odd rows (k rows) from right to left and even rows (p rows) from left to right, and rep 6-st pat rep 12 (13, 14) times, beg and ending as indicated on chart for chosen size.

Cont in pat foll chart until Back measures 5½ (6, 7½)", ending with a RS row.

Place markers at each end of last row for armholes.**

Cont in pat until Back measures 10 (11, 13)" from beg, ending with a RS row.

Shoulder Shaping

Keeping chart pat correct, bind off 22 (25, 28) sts at beg of next 2 rows. Leave rem 28 (30, 32) sts on a st holder for back neck.

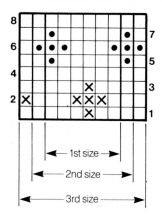

Sweater motif

KEY
☐ A
☒ B
⊡ C

FRONT

Work as for Back from ** to **.

Cont in pat foll chart until Front measures 8½ (9½, 11½)" from beg, ending with a RS row.

Neck Shaping

Next row Work first 26 (30, 34) sts in chart pat, k2tog, turn leaving rem sts on a spare needle.

Cont in pat on these sts only, dec one st at neck edge on every row until 22 (25, 28) sts rem.

Work even in pat for 4 (3, 2) rows, so ending with a RS row.

Bind off.

With RS facing, slip first 16 sts on spare needle onto a st holder, rejoin yarn to rem sts, k2 tog, work in pat to end.

Cont in pat dec one st at neck edge on every row until 22 (25, 28) sts rem.

Work even in pat until Front matches Back to shoulder shaping, ending with a WS row. Bind off.

SLEEVES

Using size 2 needles and A, cast on 56 (58, 60) sts.

Work in k1, p1 rib for ¾", inc 5 sts evenly across last row. 60 (62, 64) sts.

Change to size 3 needles and work 6 rows in stripe pat as for Back. Work in pat foll chart, rep 6-st pat rep 10 times, beg and ending as indicated on chart for chosen size, *and at the same time* shape sides by inc one st at each end of next and every foll 3rd row until there are 72 (78, 84) sts taking inc sts into pat. Work 0 (0, 2) rows in pat. Bind off.

NECKBAND

Join right shoulder seam.

With RS facing and using size 2 needles and A, pick up and k9 sts down left front neck, k16 from st holder dec one st, pick up and k11 sts up right front neck, and k28 (30, 32) sts from back st holder dec one st. 62 (64, 66) sts.

Work ¾" in k1, p1 rib, ending with a RS row.

Bind off in rib.

BUTTON BORDER

With RS facing and using size B crochet hook and A, work 2 rows of sc along left back shoulder edge.

BUTTONHOLE BORDER

With RS facing and using size B crochet hook and A, work one row of sc along left front shoulder. Then on next row, work in sc working 3 buttonhole chain loops, the first to come ¾" from shoulder edge and the last at center of neckband and rem midway between. Buttonhole chain loops are worked as foll:

Ch3, skip next sc, then cont in sc to next buttonhole.

FINISHING

Do not press.

Join side seam to underarm markers. Join sleeve seams and insert Sleeves overlapping button and buttonhole borders. Sew on buttons.

SHORT PANTS

FRONT

*Using size 3 needles and A, cast on 28 (30, 34) sts and work in k1, p1 rib for 6 rows.

Beg with a k row, work 8 rows in St st*. Leave sts on a st holder.

Work 2nd leg as for first from * to *, then k across 28 (30, 34) sts of 2nd leg, cast on 8 sts, k across 28 (30, 34) sts of first leg.**

Work even in St st on these 64 (68, 76) sts for 5½ (6½, 7)", ending with a p row. Work 6 rows in k1, p1 rib. Bind off loosely in rib.

BACK

Work as for Front from * to **.

Work even in St st on these 64 (68, 76) sts for 5 (6, 6½)", ending with a p row.

Back Shaping

Next 2 rows Work to last 5 (7, 11) sts, turn.

Next 2 rows Work to last 8 (10, 14) sts, turn.

Next 2 rows Work to last 11 (13, 17) sts, turn.

Next 2 rows Work to last 14 (16, 20) sts, turn.

Next 2 rows Work to last 17 (19, 23) sts, turn.

Next 2 rows Work to last 20 (22, 26) sts, turn.

Work 2 rows across all 64 (68, 76) sts, ending with a p row.

Work 6 rows in k1, p1 rib.
Bind off loosely in rib.

FINISHING

Do not press.
Join side and leg seams. Join elastic into a ring and pin to WS of waistband. Work a herringbone stitch casing over elastic.

BIB

TO MAKE

Using size B crochet hook and A, ch20.
1st row * 1hdc in 3rd ch from hook, *1hdc in next ch, rep from * to end. 19 sts.
2nd row Ch2 to count as first hdc, 2hdc in first hdc, *1hdc in next hdc, rep from * to end, 3hdc in 2nd of 2 ch. 23 sts.
Rep last row 5 times. 43 sts.
Cont in hdc throughout, inc one st at each end of next 2 rows. 47 sts.
Work even in hdc for 2 rows.
Dec one st at each end of next row and then on every other row 3 times more. 37 sts.
Work even for one row.

Neck Shaping
Next row Work 15 sts, turn leaving rem 22 sts unworked.
Cont on these sts only, dec one st at neck edge on every row 6 times in all. 9 sts. Fasten off.
Skip 7 sts at center neck, rejoin yarn to next st and work to end of row.
Complete to match first side, reversing shaping.

FINISHING

Using size B crochet hook and A and with RS facing, rejoin yarn to left shoulder edge and work one round of sc all around edge of Bib.
Next round 1 sc in next st, *ch3, 1 sl st in last sc, 1sc in each of next 3 sts, rep from * to end of round. Fasten off.
Cut ribbon in half and attach one piece to each shoulder edge at neck. Embroider as desired.

Baby Sleeping Bag, Cap, and Pillow

Wee Willie Winkie

Wee Willie Winkie runs through the town,
Upstairs and downstairs in his night-gown.
Rapping at the window, crying through the lock,
Are the children all in bed, for it's past 8 o' clock?

Baby Sleeping Bag, Cap, and Pillow

MATERIALS

Pingouin *Pingofrance* or other
sport yarn:
15¾oz in Blue (A)
1¾oz each in Yellow (B), Green
(C), Pink (D), and White (E)
22in open-ended zipper
6 buttons
Stuffing for pillow
One pair each of sizes 3 and 5
needles *or size to obtain correct
gauge*
Size D crochet hook

MEASUREMENTS

To fit approx 8-18 months
Finished chest measurement 32½″
Bag length 24½″
Sleeve seam 7½″

GAUGE

26 sts and 28 rows to 4″ over St st
using size 5 needles
Take time to check gauge.

ABBREVIATIONS

See page 10 for abbreviations.

SLEEPING BAG

BACK

Using size 5 needles and A, cast on
106 sts and work in St st for ¾″,
ending with a WS row.
Next row (RS) K6, *bind off 3 sts,
k15 including st already on needle,
rep from*, ending last rep k7
instead of k15.
Next row Purl, casting on 3 sts over
those bound off.
Cont in St st until Back measures 4″
from beg, ending with a p row.
Beg with a k row, cont in St st foll
chart to row 167. Bind off.

LEFT FRONT

Using size 5 needles and A, cast on
53 sts. Beg with a k row, work in St
st foll chart to row 167. Bind off.

RIGHT FRONT

Work as for Left Front, but foll other
side of chart.

SLEEVES

Using size 3 needles and A, cast on
39 sts. Work in rib as foll:
1st rib row (RS) K1,*p1, k1, rep

from * to end.
2nd rib row P1,*k1, p1, rep from *
to end.
Rep last 2 rows five times more and
first row again.
Inc row Rib 1, [insert tip of
left-hand needle under horizontal
strand before next st and knit into
back of it — called m1—, rib1]
twice, [m1, rib 2] 17 times, [m1,
rib1] twice. 60 sts.
Change to size 5 needles and beg
with a k row, work in St st foll chart
to row 43.
Make 2nd Sleeve in same way.

COLLAR

Join shoulders. With RS facing and
using size 3 needles and A, pick up
and k98 sts around neck. Work in
k1, p1 rib for 3½″. Bind off.

FINISHING

Set in Sleeves. Join sleeve and side
seams. Using crochet hook and A,
work one row of sc along side
edges and cast-on edges of flap on
Back and along cast-on edges of
each Front. Sew on buttons 1½″
from edge. Insert zipper. Work
embroidery foll chart.

CAP

TO MAKE

Using size 3 needles and A, cast on
89 sts. Work 6 rows in k1, p1 rib as
for Sleeves. Change to size 5
needles and beg with a k row, work
in St st foll chart to row 96. Bind off.

FINISHING

Join back seam and gather top of
cap. Make a pompon with A and
sew to top of cap. Work embroidery
foll chart.

PILLOW

TO MAKE

Using size 5 needles and A, cast on
106 sts and beg with a k row, work
in St st foll chart for Back for 8″.
Bind off. Make 2nd piece in same
way. Work embroidery foll chart.
Join pieces and stuff. Work 10
fringe knots in alternate colors
across short ends and trim to 1½″.

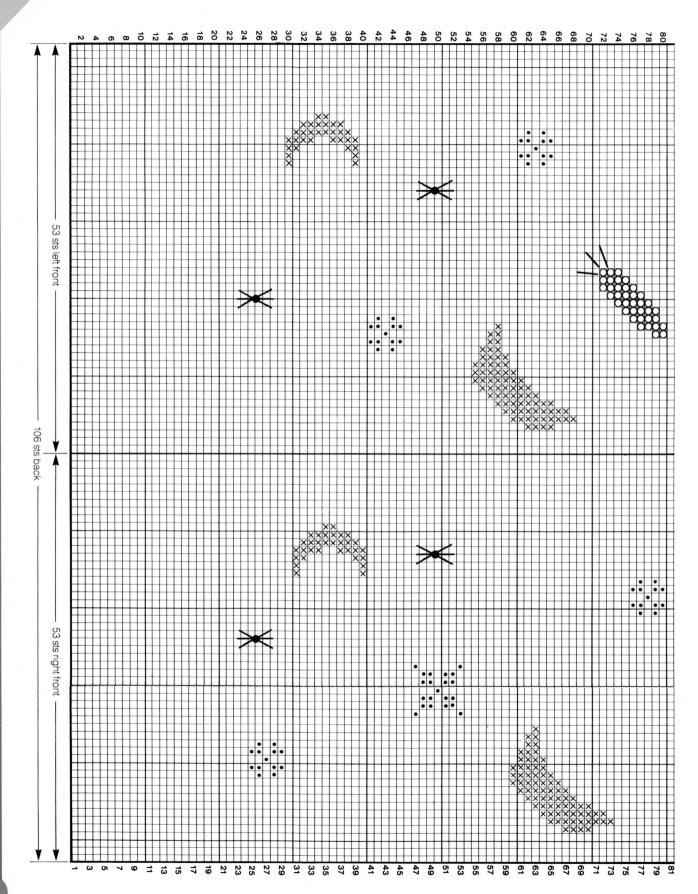

Baby sleeping bag front and back

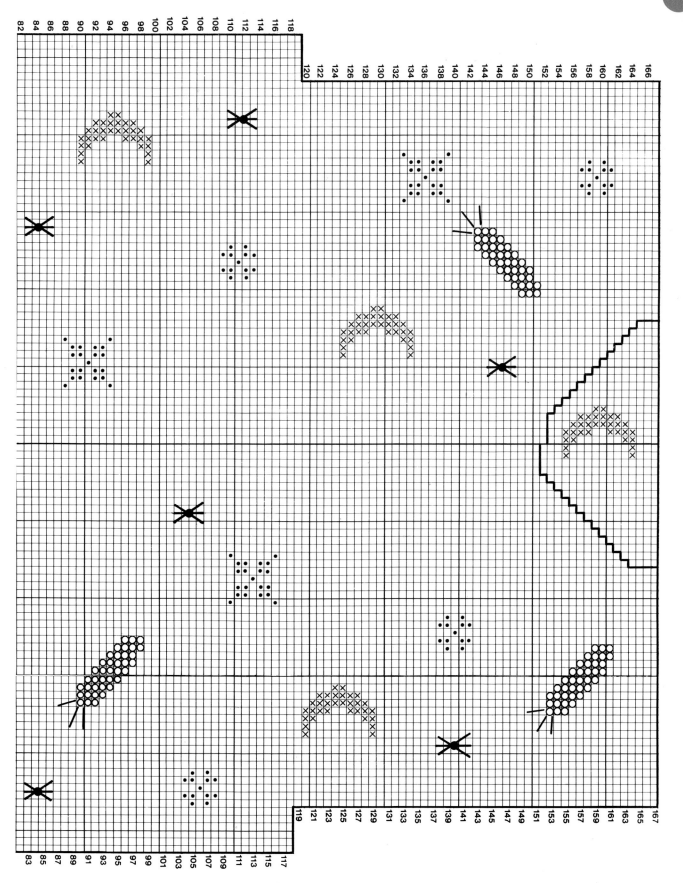

See page 40 for detailed key

Baby sleeping bag front and back

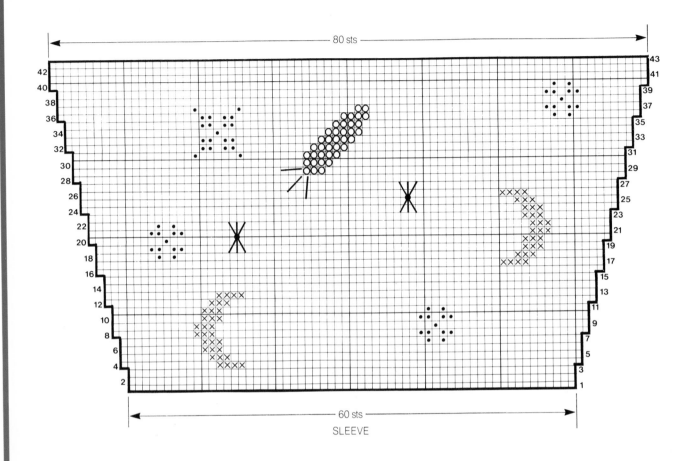

KEY

☐ = A
☒ = B
◎ = C
⊡ = D

EMBROIDERY

✳ = 6 straight stitches
and a French knot
in E

╱ = straight stitches
in C

Cap

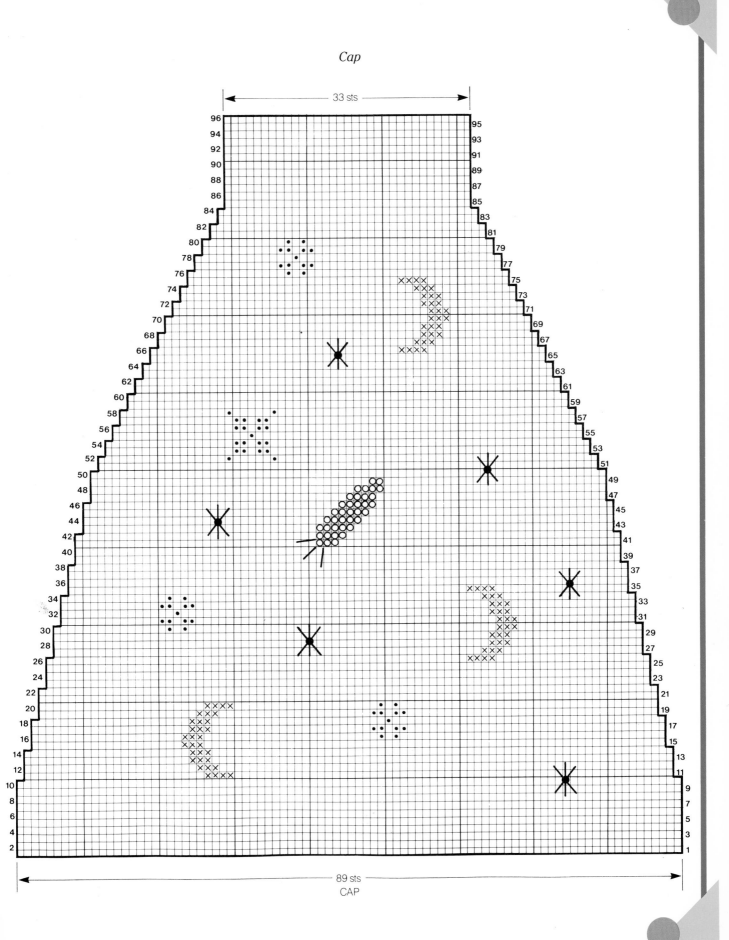

Bobby Shafto

Bobby Shafto's gone to sea,
Silver buckles on his knee;
He'll come back and marry me,
Bonny Bobby Shafto.

Child's Sailor Suit with Toy Boat

MATERIALS
Copley *Sonata DK* or other sport yarn:
7oz in Navy (A)
3½oz in White (B)
1¾oz in Red (C)
3 buttons

Waist length of elastic for pants
Stuffing for toy boat
One pair each of sizes 3 and 6 needles *or size to obtain correct gauge*

MEASUREMENTS
To fit approx 8 (12, 18) months
Finished chest measurement 20¾ (23, 25)"
Sweater length 10½ (11½, 13)"

Sleeve seam 7 (8, 8¾)"
Pants length 9¾ (10½, 11¾)"

GAUGE
22 sts and 30 rows to 4" over St st using size 6 needles
To save time, take time to check gauge.

ABBREVIATIONS
See page 10 for abbreviations.

SWEATER

BACK

Using size 3 needles and A, cast on 51 (57, 63) sts.
1st rib row (RS) K1,* p1, k1, rep from * to end.
2nd rib row P1, *k1, p1, rep from * to end.
Rep these 2 rows until ribbing measures 1¼", inc 6 sts evenly across last row and ending with a 2nd rib row. 57 (63, 69) sts.
Change to size 6 needles and beg with a k row, work in St st, working 8 rows in B and 8 rows in A.**
Rep last 16 rows until Back measures 10½ (11½, 13)" from beg, ending with a WS row.

Shoulder Shaping
Next row (RS) Bind off 17 (19, 20) sts, k 23 (25, 29) sts including st already on needle, then slip these sts onto a st holder, bind off rem 17 (19, 20) sts.

FRONT

Work as for Back to **.
Rep the last 16 rows until Front measures 5¾ (6¼, 7)" from beg, ending with a WS row.
Keeping stripe pat correct as set throughout, divide neck opening as foll:
Next row (RS) K 26 (29, 32) sts, turn leaving rem sts on spare needle.
Cont on these sts only until Front measures 8¼ (9, 10¼)" from beg, ending with a RS row.

Neck Shaping
Dec one st at neck edge on next 6 rows, then dec one st at neck edge on every other row until there are 17 (19, 20) sts.
Work even until Front measures same as Back to shoulder. Bind off.
With RS facing, rejoin yarn to rem sts, bind off 5 sts at center front and k to end.
Complete other side of neck to match first side, reversing shaping.

SLEEVES

Using size 3 needles and A, cast on 31 (33, 37) sts and k 11 rows.
Change to size 6 needles and working in St st, rep 16 rows of stripe pat as for Back, *and at the same time* inc one st at each end of 5th row and every foll 4th row until there are 45 (53, 57) sts, then on every other row until there are 53 (57, 61) sts.
Work even in pat until Sleeve measures 7 (8, 8¾)" from beg. Bind off.
Make 2nd Sleeve in same way.

BUTTONBAND

With RS facing and using size 3 needles and A, pick up and k15 (17, 19) sts evenly down left front neck edge from beg of neck shaping to bound-off sts at center.
Beg with a 2nd rib row work 7 rows in k1, p1 rib as for Back.
Bind off in rib.

BUTTONHOLE BAND

With RS facing and using size 3 needles and A, pick up and k15 (17, 19) sts up right front neck edge.
Beg with a 2nd rib row work 3 rows of k1, p1 rib as for Back, so ending with a WS row.
Work buttonholes as foll:
Next row Rib 1 (3, 3), *yo, sl 1-k1-psso, rib 3 (3, 4), rep from* once more, you, sl1-k1-psso, rib 2.
Work 3 rows more in rib.
Bind off in rib.

COLLAR

Join shoulder seams.
With RS facing and using size 3 needles and C, beg at center of Buttonhole Band and pick up and k4 sts across rem row ends of Buttonhole Band, 14 (15, 17) sts up right front neck shaping, k23 (25, 29) sts from back neck st holder, pick up and k14 (15, 17) sts down left front neck shaping and 4 sts across Button Band to center of band. 59 (63, 71) sts.
Work ¾" in k1, p1 rib as for Back, ending with a 2nd rib row.
Next row Rib 18 (19, 21) sts, insert tip of left-hand needle under horizontal strand before next st and knit into back of it — called m1 —, rib to last 18 (19, 21) sts, m1, rib to end. 61 (65, 73) sts.
Next row Rib to end, purling both increased sts.
Rep last 2 rows 7 times more, working extra sts into rib. 75 (79, 87) sts.
Bind off in rib.

FINISHING

Weave in all loose ends. Place Buttonhole Band over Button Band and sew ends to bound-off sts at center front neck.
Place markers 4¾ (5, 5½)" down side edges from shoulder seam on Back and Front. Sew Sleeves into position between markers.
Sew side and sleeve seams. Sew on buttons to correspond with buttonholes.
Fold collar in half to RS.

PANTS

RIGHT LEG

Using size 3 needles and A, cast on 53 (57, 59) sts. K 7 rows.
Change to size 6 needles and work in St st, inc one st at each end of 3rd row and every foll 3rd row until there are 61 (69, 73) sts, then every other row until there are 71 (75, 79) sts.
Work even in St st until Leg measures 3½ (4, 4½)" from beg, ending with a WS row.**

Leg Shaping
Next row Bind off 2 sts, work to end.
Next row Bind off 3 sts, work to end.
Next row Bind off 1 st, work to end.
Next row Bind off 2 sts, work to end.
Next row Bind off 1 st, work to end.
Next row Bind off 1 st, work to end. 61 (65,69) sts.
Work even until Leg measures 9 (9½, 11)" from beg, ending with a WS row.
Change to size 3 needles and work 1¾" in k1, p1 rib as for Back.
Bind off in rib.

LEFT LEG

Work as for Right Leg to **, but ending with a RS row. Then complete as for Right Leg.

FINISHING

Weave in all loose ends. Join leg seams and back and front body seams. Fold waistband in half to

KEY

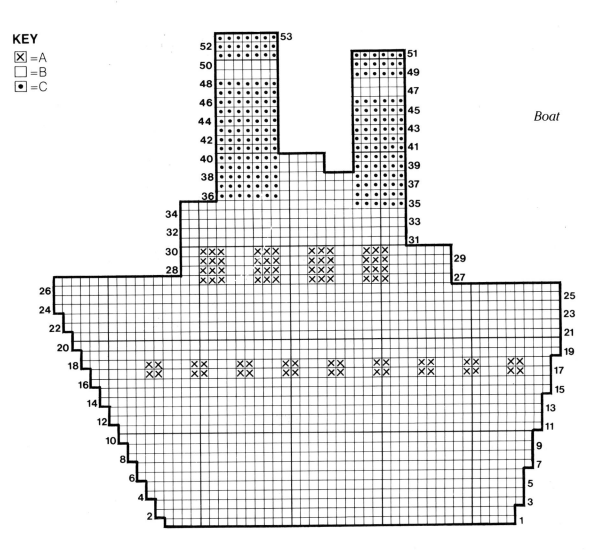

☒ =A
☐ =B
☉ =C

Boat

WS and sew in place, leaving 1¼"
open to insert elastic. Thread
elastic through waistband and
fasten firmly tog. Sew down rem
1¼" of waistband.

BOAT

FRONT
Using size 6 needles and B, cast on
39 sts. Work from chart for colors,
shaping as foll:
1st row (RS) K.
2nd row Cast on one st, p to end.
40 sts.
3rd row Cast on one st, k to end. 41
sts.
4th row As 2nd row. 42 sts.
5th-20th rows Rep first to 4th rows
4 times more. 54 sts.
21st row K.
22nd row As 2nd row. 55 sts.

23rd-24th rows Rep 21st to 22nd
rows once.
25th row K.
26th row P.
27th row Bind off 12 sts, k to end.
44 sts.
28th row Bind off 14 sts, p to end.
30 sts.
29th row K.
30th row P.
31st row Bind off 5 sts, k to end. 25
sts.
32nd row P.
33rd row K.
34th row P.
35th row K.
36th row Bind off 4sts, p to end. 21
sts.
37th row K.
38th row P.
39th row K6 sts and then slip these
sts onto a st holder, bind off 3 sts, k

to end.
Cont on these 12 sts only.
40th row P.
41st row Bind off 5 sts, k to end. 7
sts.
42nd-53rd rows Beg with a p row,
work 12 rows in St st.
Bind off.
With WS facing, rejoin yarn to 6 sts
on st holder and work even in St st
for 12 rows. Bind off.

BACK
Work as for Front, reversing
shaping by working k rows as p,
and p rows as k.

FINISHING
Weave in all loose ends.
Sew Back and Front tog, leaving an
opening of 2" at center of cast-on
edge. Stuff and sew rem 2" of seam.

The Grand Old Duke of York

The Grand old Duke of York,
He had ten thousand men;
He marched them up to the top of the hill,
And he marched them down again.

Child's Sweater, Pants, and Soldier Doll

Child's Sweater, Pants, and Soldier Doll

MATERIALS

Twilleys *Supertwist DK* or other sport yarn:

10½ (14, 14)oz in Red (A)
5¼oz in Black (B)
1¾oz in Pink (C)
2 brass buttons for epaulettes
Small amount of gold thread for medal on pocket and chin strap and buttons on doll
Waist length of elastic for pants
One pair each of sizes 2, 3, and 6 needles *or size to obtain correct gauge*
Cable needle

MEASUREMENTS

To fit approx 1 (1½, 2) years
Finished chest measurement 20½ (21¾, 23¼)″
Sweater length 12 (13, 14)″
Sleeve seam 8¼ (9, 11)″
Inside leg seam 11 (14, 15)″

GAUGE

22 sts and 30 rows to 4″ over St st using size 6 needles
To save time, take time to check gauge.

ABBREVIATIONS

See page 10 for abbreviations.

SWEATER

FRONT

** Using size 3 needles and B, cast on 50 (54, 58) sts.
Work in k2, p2 rib for 1″, inc 6 sts evenly across last row. 56 (60, 64)sts.
Break off B. **
Change to size 6 needles and using A, work in pat as foll:
1st row (RS) K8 (10, 12), [p2, k6] twice, p2, k30 (32, 34).
2nd row P30 (32, 34), k2, [p6, k2] twice, p8 (10, 12).
3rd row K8 (10, 12), [p2, slip next 3 sts onto a cable needle and hold at back of work, k3, then k3 from cable needle] twice, p2, k30 (32, 34).
4th row As 2nd row.
5th row As first row.
6th row As 2nd row.
These 6 rows form pat. Cont in pat until Front measures

6 (6½, 7½)″ from beg, ending with a WS row. Mark each end of last row with a colored thread for armholes. Cont in pat until Front measures 10½ (11½, 12½)″, ending with a WS row.

Neck Shaping
Next row Work 20 (22, 24) sts in pat, k2 tog, turn leaving rem sts on a spare needle.
Cont on these sts only and working in pat as set throughout, dec one st at neck edge on every row until 17 (18, 19) sts rem. Work even until Front measures 12 (13, 14)″ from beg, ending with a WS row.

Shoulder Shaping
Keeping pat correct, bind off 8 (9, 10) sts at beg of next row.
Work one row, then bind off rem sts. With RS of work facing, slip first 12 sts onto a st holder, rejoin yarn to rem sts, k2tog, work in pat to end. Complete to match first side, reversing shaping.

BACK

Work as for Front from ** to **.
Change to size 6 needles and using A and beg with a k row, work in St st until Back matches Front to shoulder shaping, omitting neck shaping and ending with a p row.

Shoulder shaping
Bind off 8 (9, 10) sts at beg of next 2 rows, then 9 sts at beg of foll 2 rows. Leave rem 22 (24, 26) sts on a st holder for back neck.

SLEEVES

Using size 3 needles and B, cast on 34 (34, 38) sts. Work in k2, p2 rib for 1″, inc 10 sts evenly across last row. 44 (44, 48) sts. Break off B.
Change to size 6 needles and using A and beg with a k row, work in St st, inc one st at each end of 5th row and every foll 4th row until there are 60 (70, 76) sts.
Work even in St st until Sleeve measures 8¼ (9, 11)″ from beg, ending with a p row. Bind off. Make 2nd Sleeve in same way.

TURTLE NECK

Join right shoulder seam.
With RS facing and using size 6

needles and B, pick up and k14 sts down left front neck, k12 sts from front neck st holder inc 4 sts evenly, pick up and k14 sts up right front neck and then k22 (24, 26) sts from back neck st holder inc 4 (6, 4) sts evenly. 70 (74, 74) sts.
Work in k2, p2 rib for 4″.
Bind off loosely in rib.

EPAULETTES

Using size 3 needles and B, cast on 3 sts.
1st row K1, insert tip of left-hand needle under horizontal strand before next st and p into back of it—called pick up loop and p it—, k1, pick up loop and k it, k1. 5 sts.
2nd row K2, p1, k2.
3rd row K1, pick up loop and k it, p1, k1, p1, pick up loop and k it, k1. 7 sts.
4th row K1, p1, k1, p1, k1, p1, k1.
5th row K1, pick up loop and p it, k1, p1, k1, p1, k1, pick up loop and p it, k1. 9 sts.
Cont in k1, p1 rib until band fits along shoulder edge.
Bind off loosely in rib.
Make 2nd Epaulette in same way.

POCKET

Using size 3 needles and B, cast on 23 sts.
Work in rib as foll:
1st rib row K2,* p1, k1, rep from * to last st, k1.
2nd rib row K1,* p1, k1, rep from * to end.
Rep these 2 rib rows 10 times more. Bind off in rib.

FINISHING

Join left shoulder seam and turtle neck, reversing seam half way for turtle neck. Join side seams to markers. Join Sleeve seams. Set in sleeves. Sew on epaulettes. Sew one button to each Epaulette. Using gold thread, embroider medal on pocket foll diagram. Sew on pocket.

PANTS

TO MAKE
Right Leg
** Using size 3 needles and B, cast on 36 (40, 42) sts. Work in k1, p1 rib

for 1", inc 36 (38, 42) sts evenly across last row. 72 (78, 84) sts.
Change to size 6 needles and work in pat as foll:
1st pat row (RS) K34 (37, 40)A, k4B, k34 (37, 40)A.
2nd pat row P34 (37, 40)A, p4B, p34 (37, 40)A.
Cont in pat as set until Leg measures 11 (14, 15)" from beg, ending with a 2nd pat row.
Keeping pat correct throughout, shape top by binding off 3 sts at beg of next 2 rows. Work even for 4 rows. Dec one st at each end of next and every foll 5th (6th, 7th) row until 52 (58, 64) sts rem.
Work even until Leg measures 6 (7, 7½)" from bound-off sts measured down center of work, ending with a RS row. **

Back Shaping
1st row P40 (43, 46), turn.
2nd and every other row K to end.
3rd row P31 (34, 37), turn.
5th row P22 (25, 28), turn.
7th row P13 (16, 19), turn.
9th row Knit across all sts picking up loop at points where work was turned and working it tog with next st through back of loop to avoid a hole. ***
Leave sts on a st holder.

Left Leg
Work as for Right Leg from ** to **, but working one row less, so ending with a WS row instead of a RS row.
Shape Back as for Right Leg from *** to ***, but reading k for p and p for k.
Work even for one row. Do not break off yarn.

Join Legs
With RS facing and using size 3 needles and B, k across first 51 (57, 63) sts of Left Leg, k last st of Left Leg and first st of Right Leg tog, k across rem 51 (57, 63) sts of Right Leg. 103 (115, 127) sts.
Work in rib as foll:
1st rib row (WS) *P1, k1, rep from * to last st, p1.
2nd rib row *K1, p1 rep from * to last st, k1.
Rep these 2 rib rows 9 times more. Bind off loosely in rib.

Medal

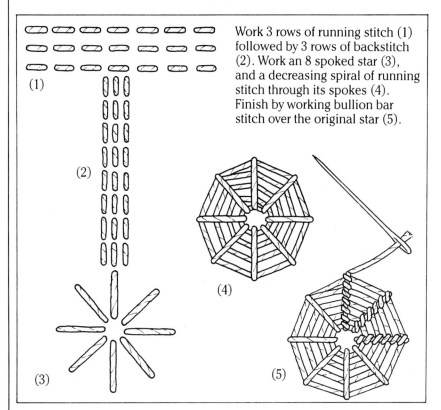

(1)
(2)
(3)
(4)
(5)

Work 3 rows of running stitch (1) followed by 3 rows of backstitch (2). Work an 8 spoked star (3), and a decreasing spiral of running stitch through its spokes (4). Finish by working bullion bar stitch over the original star (5).

FINISHING
Join leg, front and back seams. Fold waistband in half to WS and sew in place, leaving 1" open for inserting elastic. Thread elastic through waistband and fasten firmly tog. Close opening.

SOLDIER DOLL

MAIN PIECE
Beg at ankle edge and using size 2 needles and B, cast on 36 sts.
Beg with a k row and working in St st throughout, work 22 rows in B, 4 rows in A, 4 rows in B and 10 rows in A. Cont in A only, dec for shoulders as foll:
Next row K5, k2tog, k4, k2tog, k10, k2tog, k4, k2tog, k5. 32 sts.
Work even for 3 rows in A and 2 rows in C.
Cont in C only, inc for head as foll:
Next row K5, k into front and back of next st—called inc 1—, k4, inc 1, k10, inc 1, k4, inc 1, k5. 32 sts.
Work even for 21 rows in C.
Next row [K2tog] to end. 16 sts.
Break off yarn, leaving a long loose end. Thread end through rem sts.

ARMS
Beg at top of arm and using size 2 needles and A, cast on 12 sts. Beg with a k row, work 18 rows in St st.
Using B, work 4 rows in St st.
Using C, work 6 rows in St st, so ending with a WS row.
Next row [K2 tog] to end. 6 sts.
Break off yarn, thread through rem sts, pull tightly to gather, fasten off.

SHOES
Using B, cast on 8 sts and work 6 rows in St st.
Cont in St st throughout, inc one st at each end of next row.
Work even for 3 rows.
Inc one st at each end of next row.
Work even for 9 rows.
Dec one st at each end of next row.
Work even for 3 rows.
Dec one st at each end of next row.
Work even for 5 rows. Bind off.
Make 2nd Shoe in same way.

HAT
Using size 2 needles and B, cast on 50 sts.
Beg with a k row, work 22 rows in St st, so ending with a WS row.

Next row [K3, k2tog] to end. 40 sts.
Next row P.
Next row [K2, k2tog] to end. 30 sts.
Next row P.
Next row [K1, k2tog] to end. 20 sts.
Next row P.
Next row [K2tog] to end. 10 sts.
Break off yarn, thread through rem sts, pull tightly to gather, fasten off.

FINISHING

Main Piece
At the cast-on edge of the Main Piece mark position of the exact center of the row with a contrasting thread. Join row ends of the main piece, then turn right side out. Join the marked center front point of cast-on edge to the center back seam. Cont sewing back and forth through doll at the center position for 2½" up the body to form the legs. Stuff body and head through opening at top of head, then stuff legs through lower edges. Pull up length of yarn tightly at top of head and fasten off. To shape neck, tie a length of matching yarn tightly around lower edge of head, then sew ends into body.

Face
Work two stitches in A for mouth forming a V shape ½" up from the neck. Embroider eyes in B and nose in A. Join the row ends of each arm, leaving the cast-on edges open. Turn right side out and stuff. Sew the top edges of each arm tog, then sew top of arms to each side of the body ¼" down from neck.

Shoes
Bring cast-on and bound-off edges of each shoe tog and join the edges, rounding off the corners and leaving gap for turning. Turn right side out and stuff firmly, then join the gap. Place a shoe under the open end of each leg having shoes at right angles to legs. Sew ankle edge of legs to shoes.

Hat
Join row ends of hat, noting that rev St st side of work is RS. Stuff top of hat, then sew cast-on edge to head as shown. Make chin strap with gold thread, then embroider gold buttons and belt buckle.

Ride a Cock-Horse

Ride a cock-horse to Banbury Cross
To see a fine lady upon a white horse,
Rings on her fingers and bells on her toes,
And she shall have music wherever she goes.

Child's Pants and Sweater Set with Knitted Horse

Sweater

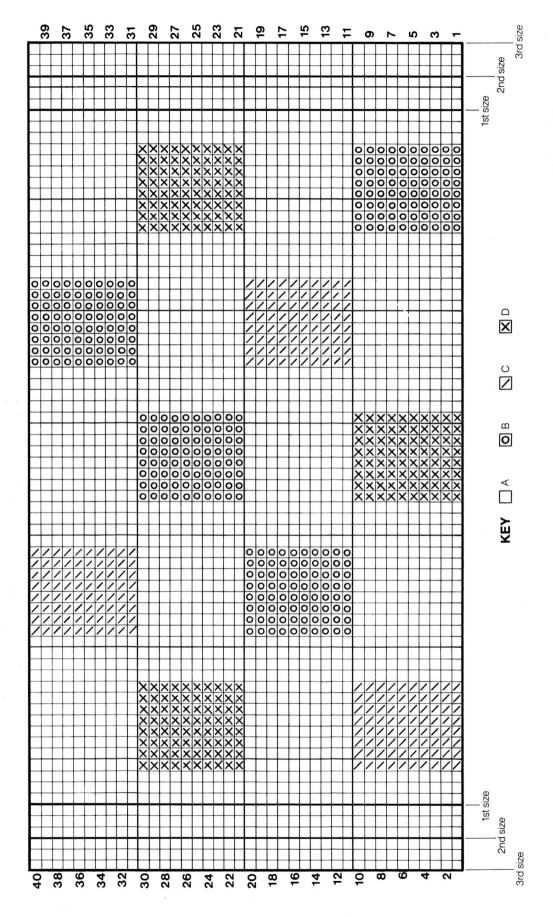

KEY ☐ A ◉ B ◪ C ☒ D

Sleeve

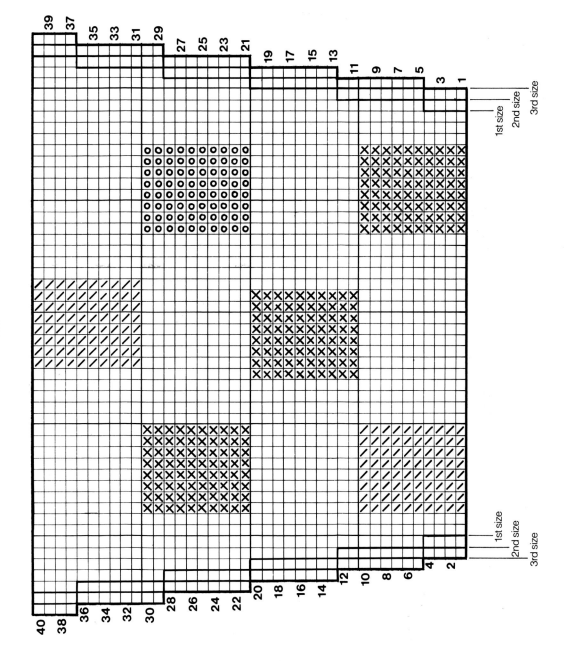

Child's Pants and Sweater Set with Knitted Horse

MATERIALS
Wendy *Family Choice DK* or other sport yarn:

Sweater and Pants
7 (8¾, 8¾)oz in Red (A)
1¾oz each in Green (B), Yellow (C), and White (D)

Horse
1¾oz each in Red (A), White (D), and Dark Brown (E)
4 buttons
Piece of wooden doweling and stuffing for horse
One pair of sizes 3 and 6 needles *or size to obtain correct gauge*

MEASUREMENTS
To fit approx 1½ (2, 3) years
Finished chest measurement 22½ (24¾, 27)"
Sweater length 10½ (11½, 12½)"
Sleeve seam 7½ (8½, 9½)"
Inside leg seam 10 (11, 13)"

GAUGE
22 sts and 30 rows to 4" over pat using size 6 needles
To save time, take time to check gauge.

ABBREVIATIONS
See page 10 for abbreviations.

SWEATER

BACK
Using size 3 needles and A, cast on 60 (66, 72) sts. Work 12 rows in k1, p1 rib, inc one st at each end of last row. 62 (68, 74) sts.
Change to size 6 needles and beg with a k row, work in St st foll chart, using separate lengths of yarn for each isolated area of colour, beg and ending as indicated for chosen size and beg again at row 1 when 40th row has been completed, until Back measures 7 (7¾, 8½)" from beg, ending with a WS row.

Armhole Shaping
Keeping to patt throughout, bind off 2 sts at beg of next 2 rows. Dec one st at each end of next row and then every other row 0 (1, 2) times more. 56 (60, 64) sts.
Work even until armhole measures 3½ (3¾, 4)", ending with a WS row.

Shoulder Shaping
Bind off 7 (7, 8) sts at beg of next 2 rows and then 7 (8, 8) sts at beg of foll 2 rows. Leave rem 28 (30, 32) sts on a st holder.

FRONT
Work as for Back until armhole measures 2½ (2¾, 3)", ending with a WS row.

Neck Shaping
Next row K20 (22, 23) sts in pat, turn leaving rem sts on a spare needle.
Cont on these sts only and working in pat throughout, dec one st at neck edge of every row until 14 (15, 16) sts rem. Work even until armhole measures same as Back to shoulder, ending with a WS row. Bind off 7 (7, 8) sts at beg of next row. Work even for one row. Bind off rem sts. Return to rem sts and with RS facing slip center 14 (16, 18) sts onto a st holder, rejoin yarn to rem sts and complete to match first side, reversing shaping.

SLEEVES
Using size 3 needles and A, cast on 38 (40, 42) sts and work in k1, p1 rib for 16 rows. Change to size 6 needles and beg with a k row, work in St st foll sleeve chart *and at the same time* inc one st at each end of 5th and every foll 8th row until there are 48 (50, 52) sts. Work even in pat until Sleeve measures 7½ (8½, 9½)", ending with a WS row.

Cap Shaping
Keeping to pat throughout, bind off 2 sts at beg of next 2 rows. Dec one st at each end of next row and then on every other row 1 (2, 3) times more. Bind off 2 sts at beg of next 10 rows. Bind off 3 sts at beg of next 4 rows. Bind off rem 8 sts. Make 2nd Sleeve in same way.

NECKBAND
Join right shoulder seam. With RS facing and using size 3 needles and A, pick up and k14 sts down left front neck, 14 (16, 18) sts across center front, 14 sts up right front neck and k28 (30, 32) from back neck st holder. 70 (74, 78) sts. Work in k1, p1 rib for 5 rows. Bind off in rib.

FINISHING
Join left shoulder, leaving 1" open at neck edge. Join side and sleeve seams. Set in Sleeves. Work sc along neck opening. Make 2 button loops on front left shoulder. Sew buttons to back left shoulder loops.

PANTS

LEGS
Using size 3 needles and A, cast on 52 (56, 60) sts and work 16 rows in stripes in k1, p1 rib as foll:
4 rows A, 2 rows B, 2 rows C, 2 rows D, 2 rows C, 2 rows B, 2 rows A.
Cont in A only.
Next row K0 (2, 4), [k into front and back of next st, k1] 26 times, k0 (2, 4). 78 (82, 86) sts.
Change to size 6 needles and beg with a p row, work in St st until Leg measures 5 (5½, 6½)" from beg, ending with a WS row.
Cont in St st, inc one st at each end of next and then every 6th row until there are 86 (90, 94) sts.
Work even until Leg measures 9 (11, 13)" from beg, ending with a WS row. Leave sts on a st holder. Work a 2nd Leg in same way.

Join Legs
With RS facing and using size 6 needles and A, work across 2nd Leg first, k2tog, k82 (86, 90) sts, k2tog, then work across first Leg in same way. 168 (176, 184) sts.
** Cont in St st, work even for 3 rows, so ending with a WS row.
Next row K to center 4 sts, (k2tog) twice, k to end.** 166 (174, 182) sts.
Work even for 3 rows.
Next row *K2tog, k79 (83, 87), k2tog, rep from * once. 162 (170, 178) sts.
Rep from ** to ** once. 160 (168, 176) sts.
Work even for 3 rows, dec one st at each end of next row, work even for 7 rows, dec one st at each end of next row. 156 (164, 172) sts.
Work even until piece measures 7¾ (8½, 9)" from crotch, ending with a WS row. Dec 22 sts evenly across

next row. 134 (142, 150) sts.
Change to size 3 needles and work
in k1, p1 rib for 5 rows.
Next row Rib 52 (56, 60), bind off 3
sts, rib 24, bind off 3 sts, rib to end.
Next row Work in rib, casting on 3
sts over those bound off.
Work 3 rows in rib and bind off.

STRAPS
Using size 3 needles and A, cast on
7 sts. Work in k1, p1 rib until Strap
measures 11 (13, 15)″. Bind off.
Make 2nd Strap in same way.

FINISHING
Join back and leg seams. Sew on
straps and buttons.

HORSE

FIRST SIDE OF HEAD
Using size 6 needles and D, cast on
45 sts. Beg with a k row, work in St
st for 6 rows, so ending with a WS
row. Cont in St st throughout, inc
one st at end of next row.
** Work even for 3 rows, so ending
with a WS row. Inc one st at end of
next row.** Rep from ** to ** once
more. 48 sts. Work even for 3 rows.
*** Dec one st at beg and inc one st
at end of next row. Work one row.
Dec one st at beg of next row. Work
one row.***
Rep from *** to *** once more.
Dec one st at beg and inc one st at
end of next row. Work one row, so
ending with a WS row. 46 sts. Leave
these neck sts on a st holder, but do
not break off yarn. Using size 6
needles and D, cast on 8 sts for
nose.
1st row K.
2nd row P, inc one st at beg of row.
3rd row Cast on 5 sts, k to end.
4th row P.
5th row K, inc one st at beg of row.
6th row P, inc one st at end of row.
7th–14th rows Rep 5th and 6th
rows 4 times. 24 sts.
15th row K, inc one st at beg and
dec one st at end of row.
16th row As 6th row. 25 sts.
17th–20th rows Rep 5th and 6th
rows twice. 29 sts. Break off yarn.
Join neck and nose sections as foll:
Working across neck, k2tog, k44,
then cast on 2 sts and k nose sts,
dec one st at end of row. 75 sts.
Purl one row, k one row dec one st

at beg. Rep last 2 rows once. Purl
one row. K one row dec one st at
each end, then p one row.
Rep last 2 rows until 59 sts rem.
Cont in St st, dec one st at beg of
every k row and end of every other k
row until 49 sts rem, so ending with
a RS row.
P one row dec one st at end, then k
one row dec one st at each end.
Rep last 2 rows once. Dec one st at
each end of next 4 rows.
Bind off 3 sts at beg of next 4 rows.
Bind off 5 sts at beg of next 2 rows.
Bind off rem sts.

SECOND SIDE OF HEAD
Work as for first side, but reversing
all shaping.

EARS
Using size 6 needles and D, cast on
3 sts. Beg with a k row, work in St st
inc one st at each end of every k
row until there are 15 sts. Cont in St
st, work even for 6 rows.
Next row K6, sl 1-k2tog-psso, k6.
Next row P.
Next row K5, sl 1-k2tog-psso, k5.

Next row P.
Cont in this way dec 2 sts at center
of every RS row until 3 sts rem.
P3tog. Bind off. Make 3 more ear
pieces in same way.

BRIDLE AND MOUTH PIECE
Using size 6 needles and A, cast on
5 sts. Work in St st for 14″. Bind off.
Make 3 more Straps in same way,
one 8″ and two 4″ long.

FINISHING
Join both sides of head tog. Sew ear
pieces tog. Cut a thin piece of
cardboard to the shape of ear and
insert before sewing ears to head.
Using E, embroider eyes and
nostrils. Cut 10″ strands of E and
thread along back of neck for
mane. Sew short ends of neck and
head bridle tog to form rings. Sew
short pieces to side and stitch
bridle to neck. Stuff horse's head.
Fold neck into small pleats and
secure the head onto the doweling
with upholstery tacks. Make 3 more
pieces as for Straps 26″ long. Tie
tog in a ribbon over tacks.

Little Boy Blue

Little Boy Blue,
Come blow your horn,
The sheep's in the meadow,
The cow's in the corn.

All-In-One Suit, Mittens, and Socks

MATERIALS
Pingouin *Pingofrance* or other sport yarn:
12¼oz in Light Blue (A)
3½oz in Mid Blue (B)
Small amount each in Gold (C), Green (D), and Purple (E)
12 (14)" zipper
One pair each of sizes 3 and 5 needles *or size to obtain correct gauge*
Set of four size 3 double-pointed needles
Size D crochet hook

MEASUREMENTS
To fit approx 1½-2 years (2-3)
Finished chest measurement 22 (23¾)" Length (from shoulder to crotch) 13 (15)"
Sleeve seam 8 (8½)"

GAUGE
26 sts and 32 rows to 4in" over pat using size 5 needles
To save time, take time to check gauge.

ABBREVIATIONS
See page 10 for abbreviations.

SUIT

BODY
Left Leg
Using size 3 needles and A, cast on 49 (51) sts.
Work in rib as foll:
1st rib row (RS) K1, *p1, k1, rep from * to end.
2nd rib row P1, *k1, p1, rep from * to end.
Rep last 2 rows for 3", ending with a RS row.
Next row (WS) P1 (0), p into front and back of every st to last 1 (0) st, p1 (0). 96 (102) sts.
Change to size 5 needles and work in basket weave pat as foll:
1st row (RS) K.
2nd row P.
3rd row K1, *p4, k2, rep from *, ending last rep with k1 instead of k2.
4th row P1, *k4, p2, rep from *, ending last rep with p1 instead of p2.
5th row As 3rd row.
6th row As 4th row.
7th row K.
8th row P.
9th row P2, *k2, p4, rep from *, ending last rep with p2 instead of p4.

10th row K2, *p2, k4, rep from *, ending last rep with k2 instead of k4.

11th row As 9th row.

12th row As 10th row.

These 12 rows form the basket weave pat. Work in pat until Leg measures 11 (12)″ from beg, ending with a WS row.

Crotch Shaping

Keeping pat correct, bind off 2 sts at beg of next 2 rows, then dec one st at each end of next row, work even for one row and dec one st at each end of next row. 88 (94) sts. Keeping patt correct, work even until Leg measures 19 (19½)″ from beg, ending with a first or 7th pat row. **

Break off yarn and leave sts on a spare needle.

Right Leg

Work as for Left Leg to **. Do not break off yarn.

Next row (WS) *P0 (3), [p3, p2tog] 17 times, p3 (6)*, then rep from * to * across Left Leg.
142 (154) sts.

Change to size 3 needles and work 6 rows in k1, p1 rib, so ending with a WS row.

Change to size 5 needles and work in pat as foll:

1st row (RS) *P4, k2, rep from * to last 4 sts, p4.

2nd row *K4, p2, rep from * to last 4 sts, k4.

3rd row As first row.

4th row As 2nd row.

5th row K.

6th row P.

7th row P1, *k2, p4, rep from * to last 3 sts, k2, p1.

8th row K1, *p2, k4, rep from * to last 3 sts, p2, k1.

9th row As 7th row.

10th row As 8th row.

Right Front

Divide for Fronts and Back on next row as foll:

Next row (RS) K36 (39) sts, turn leaving rem 106 (115) sts on a spare needle for Back and Left Front. Cont on these 36 (39) sts for Right Front and shape armhole as foll:

Next row Bind off 3 sts (armhole edge), p to end.

Keeping pat correct, dec one st at armhole edge of next 2 RS rows. 31 (34) sts.

*** Work even in pat as now set until piece measures 22½ (25½)″ from beg, ending at front edge.

Neck Shaping

Keeping pat correct throughout, bind off at neck edge on next and every other row 6 (7) sts once, 3 sts once, 2 sts twice, then dec one st at neck on every other row twice. 16 (18) sts.

Work even until piece measures 24 (27)″ from beg, ending with a WS row.
Bind off.

Back

With RS facing, slip first 70 (76) sts from spare needle onto a size 5 needle, leaving rem 36 (39) sts on spare needle for Left Front.
Rejoin A and cont on center 70 (76) sts shaping armholes as foll:
Beg with a RS row and keeping pat correct throughout, bind off 3 sts at beg of next 2 rows, then dec one st at each end of next row, work even for one row and dec one st at each end of next row. 60 (66) sts.
Work even until Back measures same as Right Front to shoulder, ending with a WS row.
Bind off.

Left Front

Return to rem 36 (39) sts and with RS facing, rejoin A and shape armhole of Left Front as foll:
Keeping pat correct, bind off 3 sts at beg of next row (armhole edge), then dec one st at armhole edge of next 2 RS rows. 31 (34) sts.
Work as for Right Front from *** to end.

SLEEVES

Using size 3 needles and A, cast on 35 (41) sts. Work in k1, p1 rib as for Legs for 1½″, ending with a WS row and inc one st at end of last row. 36 (42) sts.
Change to size 5 needles and work 8 rows in basket weave pat as for Left Leg, then keeping pat correct throughout, inc one st at each end of next row and every foll 6th row until there are 54 (60) sts.

Work even until Sleeve measures 8 (8½)″ from beg, ending with a WS row.

Cap Shaping

Bind off 3 sts at beg of next 2 rows, then dec one st at each end of every other row twice. 44 (50) sts. Bind off.
Make 2nd Sleeve in same way.

NECKBAND

Join shoulder seams. With RS facing and using size 3 needles and A, pick up and k22 (23) sts up right front neck, 27 (29) sts across back neck and 22 (23) sts down left front neck. 71 (75) sts. Work 6 rows in k1, p1 rib. Bind off in rib.

HOOD

Using size 3 needles and A, cast on 81 (87) sts.
Work 6 rows in k1, p1 rib as for Left Leg, ending with a WS row and inc 3 sts evenly across last row. 84 (90) sts.
Change to size 5 needles and work in basket weave pat as for Left Leg for 6½ (7½)″. Bind off 31 sts at beg of next 2 rows. Cont in pat on rem 22 (28) sts until piece measures 4½″ from bind off. Bind off.
Sew the bound-off edges at each side of the Hood to sides of extension section.
With RS of Hood facing and using size 3 needles and A, pick up and k121 (125) sts evenly around front edge of Hood, beg and ending at lower edge of Hood.
Work 4 rows in k1, p1 rib as for Legs, beg with a 2nd rib row. Bind off loosely in rib.

POCKET

Using size 3 needles and D, cast on 15 sts. Beg with a k row, work in St st foll chart using D, C, and B as indicated. Bind off. Embroider grass in D and child in E as shown on chart.

FINISHING

Do not press. Set sleeves into armholes, then join side and sleeve seams. Join center front seam along crotch shaping, leaving 12 (14)″ open from neckline. Join center back seam and join inner leg

60

Knitting chart

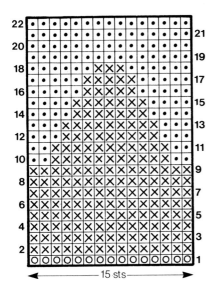

— 15 sts —

Embroidery chart

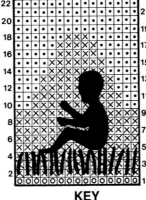

KEY

●	B
✕	C
○	D

seam. Sew cast-on edge of Hood to neck edge, sewing inside neckband so that seam is hidden. Sew on pocket. Insert zipper. Make a pompon using A and attach to the zipper pull.

MITTENS

TO MAKE

Using size 3 needles and B, cast on 27 (29) sts loosely.

1st rib row (RS) K2, *p1, k1, rep from * to last st, k1.

2nd rib row K1, *p1, k1, rep from * to end.

Rep last 2 rows 3 times more, ending with a WS row and inc one st at end of last row. 28 (30) sts. Change to size 5 needles and work slot row as foll:

Next row K1, *yo, k2tog, rep from * to last st, k1.

Beg with a p row, work 3 rows in St st.

Thumb Shaping

1st row K12 (13), k into front and back of next st—called inc 1—, k2, inc 1, k12 (13).

2nd and 4th rows K1, p to last st, k1.

3rd row K12 (13), inc 1, k4, inc 1, k12 (13).

5th row K12 (13), inc 1, k6, inc 1, k12 (13).

6th row As 2nd row. 34 (36) sts.

Thumb

Next row K13 (14) sts, slip these 13 (14) sts onto a st holder, k8, turn, slip rem 13 (14) sts onto a thread. Beg with a p row, work 7 rows in St st.

Next row [K2tog] 4 times. 4 sts. Break off yarn, thread yarn through rem sts, pull tightly and fasten off. Sew thumb seam.

With RS facing and using size 5 needle, pick up and k2 sts from base of thumb, then using same needle k 13 (14) sts left on thread.

Next row P15 (16) sts, then p13 (14) sts from st holder. 28 (30) sts. Work 6 (8) rows in St st.

Top Shaping

1st row K1, k2tog tbl, k8 (9), k2tog, k2, k2tog tbl, k8 (9), k2tog, k1.

2nd, 4th and 6th rows K1, p to last st, k1.

3rd row K1, k2tog tbl, k6 (7), k2tog, k2, k2tog tbl, k6 (7), k2tog, k1.

5th row K1, k2tog tbl, k4 (5), k2tog, k2, k2tog tbl, k4 (5), k2tog, k1.

7th row K1, k2tog tbl, k2 (3), k2tog, k2, k2tog tbl, k2 (3), k2tog, k1.

8th row As 2nd row.

Bind off rem 12 (14) sts.

Join mitten seam. Using crochet hook and B, make a length of chain 14″ long. Thread through slot at wrist. Make 2 small pompons and sew one to each end of chain. Make 2nd Mitten in same way.

SOCKS

TO MAKE

Using set of four double-pointed needles and B, cast on 36 sts, with 12 sts on each of 3 needles. Work 8 rounds in k1, p1 rib. Work in St st (k every round) for 3 (3½)″.

Divide for heel

K7 off first needle onto 3rd needle and sl one st from 2nd needle onto 3rd needle. 20 sts on 3rd needle. Divide rem 16 sts on other 2 needles.

Heel

Working 20 sts on 3rd needle, turn and p across 20 sts, turn and cont in rows, work 12 rows more in St st on these 20 sts slipping first st of every row, so ending with a p row.

Next row K10, k2tog tbl, turn.

Next row P1, p2tog, turn.

Next row K2, k2tog tbl, turn.

Next row P3, p2tog, turn.

Cont in this way knitting and purling one extra st on each row until 12 sts rem, then k8, k2tog tbl, turn p9, p2tog. 10 sts. K across these 10 sts, pick up and k9 sts down side of heel, k along sts for top of foot onto next needle and with next needle pick up and k9 sts along other side of the heel and k5 sts from flat of heel. 14 sts on first needle, 16 sts on 2nd needle, 14 sts on 3rd needle.

*Next round K.

Next round Beg at center of heel (first needle), k to last 3 sts on needle, k2tog tbl, k1; k across sts on 2nd needle for top; then k1, sl 1-k1-psso, k to end of 3rd needle.* Rep from * to * until 8 sts rem on each of first and 3rd needles. Work even until foot measures 3½″.

Toe Shaping

Next round First needle k to last 3 sts, k2tog, k1; on 2nd needle k1, sl 1-k1-psso, k to last 3 sts, k2tog, k1; on 3rd needle k1, sl 1-k1-psso, k to end.

Next round K.

Rep last 2 rounds until 16 sts rem. K4 sts from first needle onto 3rd needle, place side by side and graft sts tog to finish. Make 2nd Sock in same way.

Playsuit and Baby Toy

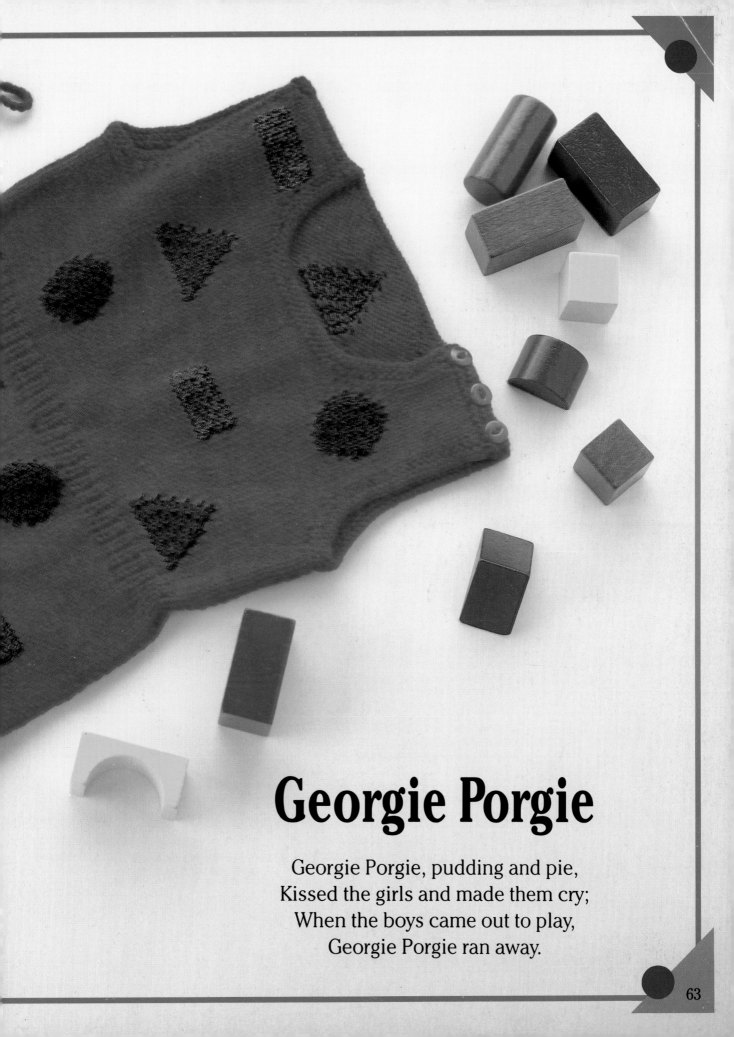

Georgie Porgie

Georgie Porgie, pudding and pie,
Kissed the girls and made them cry;
When the boys came out to play,
Georgie Porgie ran away.

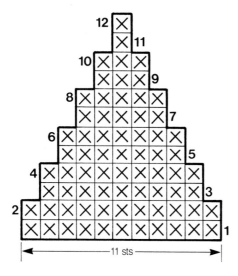

Note: Work motifs at random in colors B,C,D throughout garment.

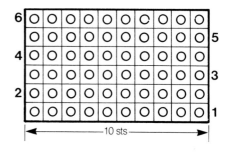

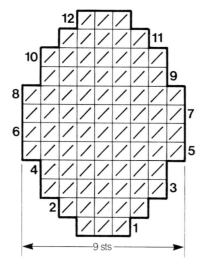

KEY

$\boxed{O}$ =B

$\boxed{/}$ =C

$\boxed{\times}$ =D

Playsuit and Baby Toy

MATERIALS
Robin *Columbine DK* or other sport yarn:
7 (7, 8¾)oz in Red (A)
1¾oz each in Jade (B), Violet (C), and Blue (D)
3 buttons
Small amounts of A, B, C, and D and stuffing for toy
One pair each of sizes 3 and 6 needles *or size to obtain correct gauge*
Size E crochet hook

MEASUREMENTS
To fit approx 1½ (2, 4) years
Finished chest measurement 23¼ (25½, 27)″
Length 23¼ (26, 29)″

GAUGE
22 sts and 30 rows to 4″ over St st using size 6 needles
Take time to check gauge.

ABBREVIATIONS
See page 10 for abbreviations.

PLAYSUIT

TO MAKE
Using size 3 needles and A, cast on 52 (56, 60) sts for Left Leg. Work 12 rows in k1, p1 rib.
Change to size 6 needles.
Next row K14 (15, 17) sts, [k into front and back of next st] 25 (27, 27) times, k13 (14, 16) sts. 77 (83, 87) sts.
Working in St st and working motifs in B,C, and D at random

throughout, work even until Leg measures 9 (10¼, 11¾)″ from beg, ending with a p row.

Crotch Shaping
Bind off 2 sts at beg of next 2 rows. Dec one st each end of next row and then every other row 3 times in all, ending with a p row. Dec one st at beg of next row and then at beg of every other row 4 times in all. 64 (70, 74) sts.
Work even until Leg measures 6 (6¾, 7½)″ from beg of crotch shaping, ending with a p row.

Back Shaping
Next row K32 (35, 38) sts, turn leaving rem sts on st holder.
P one row.
Next row K26 (29, 32) sts, turn.
P one row.
Cont in this way working 6 sts less before turning on RS rows twice more**, ending after a p row. Leave sts on a spare needle.

Right Leg
Work as Left Leg to **, reversing shaping and ending with a k row.

Bodice Back
Next row P32 (35, 37) sts, turn leaving rem sts on st holder.
Change to size 3 needles and work 32 (35, 37) sts in k1, p1 rib, then work 32 (35, 37) sts from those left on spare needle of Left Leg in rib. 64 (70, 74) sts.
Work 5 rows more in rib on these sts. Change to size 6 needles. Work even in St st and motifs until Back measures 2¼ (3, 3½)″ from top of ribbing, ending with a p row.

Armhole Shaping
Bind off 4 sts at beg of next 2 rows, dec one st each end of next row and then every other row 3 (4, 4) times in all. 50 (54, 58) sts.
Work even until armhole measures 4 (4½, 4¾)″, ending with a p row.

Neck Shaping
Next row K13 (14, 16) sts, turn leaving rem sts on a spare needle.
Cont on these sts only, dec one st at neck edge on next 2 WS rows. 11 (12, 14) sts. Work even until armhole measures 4¾ (5¼, 5½)″.

Bind off. Return to sts on spare needle and slip first 24 (26, 26) sts onto a st holder, k to end. Complete to match first side, reversing shaping.

Bodice Front
Return to sts left on st holders at completion of Legs and with RS facing and using size 3 needles and A, work in k1, p1 rib across 32 (35, 37) sts of Left Leg, then across 32 (35, 37) sts of Right Leg.
Cont as for Bodice Back until armholes measure 2½ (2½, 2¾)″, ending with a p row.

Neck Shaping
Next row K17 (18, 20) sts, turn leaving rem sts on a spare needle. Bind off 2 sts at beg of next row. Work one row. Dec one st at neck edge on next row and then every other row 4 times in all. 11 (12, 14) sts. Work even until armhole measures same as back. Bind off. Return to sts left on spare needle, slip first 16 (18, 18) sts onto a st holder, k to end. Complete to match first side, reversing shaping.

ARMHOLE BORDERS
Join side seams. Using size 3 needles and A, and with RS facing, pick up and k68 (72, 72) sts around armhole. Work 3 rows in g st. Bind off.

NECKBAND
Join right shoulder seam. Using size 3 needles and A and with RS facing, pick up and k15 (17, 18) sts down left front neck, k16 (18, 18) sts from center front st holder, pick up and k15 (17, 18) sts up right front neck, k5 sts down right back neck, k24 (26, 26) sts from back neck st holder, and pick up and k5 sts up left back neck. 80 (88, 90) sts. K 3 rows in g st. Bind off.

BUTTON BAND
Using size 3 needles and A and with RS facing, pick up and k15 (17, 19) sts along back left shoulder. Work 3 rows in g st. Bind off.

BUTTONHOLE BAND
Work as for Button Band, but picking up sts along front left

shoulder and working buttonholes on 2nd row as foll:
Buttonhole row K1, yo, k2tog, *k3 (4, 5) sts, yo, k2tog, rep from * once more, k2.

FINISHING
Join center back and front seams. Join leg seams. Sew on buttons.

BABY TOY

BALL
Using size 3 needles and C, cast on 8 sts.
1st and all WS rows P.
2nd row *K into front and back of next st—called inc—, rep from * to end. 16 sts.
4th row *K1, inc 1, rep from * to end.
6th row *K2, inc 1, rep from * to end.
8th row *K3, inc 1, rep from * to end.
Work 11 rows in St st.
20th row *K3, k2tog, rep from * to end. 32 sts.
22nd row *K2, k2tog, rep from * to end. 24 sts.
24th row *K1, k2tog, rep from * to end.
26th row *K2tog, rep from * to end. Break off yarn, thread through sts, pull tightly and fasten off. Make 2nd piece in same way. Join seam leaving an opening. Turn right side out. Stuff and close seam.

TRIANGLE
Using size 3 needles and D, cast on 18 sts. Working in St st, dec one st at each end of every 3rd row until 2 sts rem. Bind off. Make 2nd piece in same way.
For gusset cast on 5 sts and working in St st, make a strip long enough to go around 3 sides of triangle. Bind off. Sew gusset in place leaving an opening. Stuff and close seam.

RECTANGLE
Using size 3 needles and B, cast on 16 sts and work 12 rows in St st. Bind off. Make 2nd piece in same way. Work gusset and finish off as for triangle.
Link motifs tog with a crochet chain, using A double.

Little Bo Peep

Little Bo Peep has lost her sheep,
And doesn't know where to find them,
Leave them alone, and they'll come home,
Bringing their tails behind them.

Jacket, Bonnet, And Muff

Jacket, Bonnet, And Muff

MATERIALS

Copley *Sonata DK* or other sport yarn:
10½oz in Lemon (A)
3½oz in White (B)
7 buttons
2¼yd of ½" wide white ribbon
Lining and padding for muff
One pair each of sizes 3 and 6 needles *or size to obtain correct gauge*

MEASUREMENTS

To fit approx 2 (4) years
Finished chest measurement 24 (27¾)"
Length 12 (13½)"
Sleeve seam 9 (10)"

GAUGE

22 sts and 43 rows to 4" over g st using size 6 needles
Take time to check gauge.

ABBREVIATIONS

See page 10 for abbreviations.

JACKET

POCKET LININGS

Using size 6 needles and A, cast on 16 sts. Work 12 rows in g st. Leave sts on a spare needle. Make a 2nd Lining in same way.

LEFT FRONT

Using size 6 needles and A, cast on 37 (42) sts. Work 25 rows in g st.

Pocket Shaping
26th row (WS) K30 sts, turn leaving rem sts unworked.
27th row and foll RS rows K.
28th row K28 sts, turn.
30th row K26 sts, turn.
32nd row K24 sts, turn.
34th row K22 sts, turn.
36th row K20 sts, turn.
38th row K18 sts, turn.
40th row K16 sts, turn.
42nd row K14 sts, bind off next 16 sts, k rem 7 (12) sts.
Next row (RS) K7 (12) sts, k the 16 sts from first pocket lining, turn leaving rem sts unworked.
K 15 rows on these 23 (28) sts only, so ending with a WS row (at side edge).

43rd row (RS) K23 (28) sts, then k rem 14 sts. 37 (42) sts.
Work even in g st until Left Front measures 10 (11½)", ending with a RS row (at center edge).

Neck Shaping
Next row (WS) Bind off 3 (5) sts, k next 4 (6) sts including st already on right-hand needle after bind off and slip these 4 (6) sts onto a st holder, k rem 30 (33) sts.
K 4 rows, dec one st at neck edge on every row. 26 (29) sts.
K 14 rows, dec one st at neck edge on 2nd and every foll 3rd row 5 times in all. 21 (24) sts.
K 2 rows more, so ending with a WS row (at side edge).

Shoulder Shaping
Bind off 6 sts at beg of next row and then bind off 5 (6) sts at beg of every other row 3 times.

RIGHT FRONT

Mark positions of buttons on Left Front; the first 1¼" from lower edge, the last ½" from neck edge, and the rem 3 equally spaced between.
Work first 24 rows as for Left Front and at the same time work buttonholes to correspond with markers when reached as foll:
1st buttonhole row (RS) K3, k2tog, yo twice, k to end.
2nd buttonhole row (WS) K all sts except 2nd yo which should be dropped from left-hand needle after first yo has been knitted.

Pocket Shaping
25th row (RS) K30 sts, turn leaving rem sts unworked.
26th row and foll WS rows K.
27th row As 28th row for Left Front.
29th row As 30th row for Left Front.
30th row K.
Cont foll instructions for Left Front from 32nd row, noting that RS rows, are WS rows and WS rows are RS rows for Right Front.

BACK

Using size 6 needles and A, cast on 66 (76) sts. Work in g st until Back measures same as Fronts to shoulder shaping.

Shoulder Shaping
Bind off 6 sts at beg of next 2 rows and 5 (6) sts at beg of foll 6 rows.
Bind off rem 24 (28) sts for neck.

SLEEVES

Using size 3 needles and B, cast on 36 (40) sts. K one row.
Change to A and k 20 rows. This completes turn-back cuff.
Change to size 6 needles and cont in g st, inc one st at each end of next row and then every foll 7th row until there are 54 (60) sts.
Cont in g st until Sleeve measures 9 (10)" from end of cuff. Bind off.
Make 2nd Sleeve in same way.

COLLAR

Join shoulder seams.
With RS facing using size 3 needles and A, beg at center edge of Right Front and k4 (6) sts from st holder, pick up and k19 sts up right front neck, 24 (28) sts across back neck, 19 sts down left front neck, and k4 (6) sts from st holder. 70 (78) sts.
1st row K5 (3) sts, *k2tog, k3, rep from * to end. 57 (63) sts.
2nd-4th rows K.
5th row K4, insert tip of left-hand needle under horizontal strand before next st and work into back of it—called m1—, k to last 4 sts, k4.
6th-9th rows As 2nd-5th rows.
Using B, k one row and bind off.

POCKET TOPS

Using size 3 needles and A, cast on one st, then with RS facing pick up and k one st from each of the 16 sts bound off for pocket opening, cast on one st, turn. K 10 rows.
Using B, k one row and bind off.

FINISHING

Sew pocket linings to WS of Fronts. Fold down pocket tops and sew one button to center of each. Pin center of bound-off edge of each Sleeve to shoulder seam and stretching top of Sleeve slightly, pin to side edges of Front and Back and sew Sleeves in position. Sew side and sleeve seams, reversing seam for turn-back cuff. Do not press. Sew on buttons.

BONNET

TO MAKE

Using size 3 needles and A, cast on 67 (73) sts.
1st row K4, k1, *p1, k1, rep from * to last 4 sts.
2nd row K4, p1, *k1, p1, rep from * to last 4 sts, k4.
Rep these 2 rows 3 times more.
Change to size 6 needles and keeping 4 sts in g st at each end of piece, work 4½ (5)″ in St st, ending with a p row.
Keeping to pat as set, bind off 23 (25) sts, at beg of next 2 rows, so ending with a p row 21 (23) sts.

Back Panel
K one row, p one row.
Dec row K2, k2tog, k to last 4 sts, k2tog tbl, k2.
Cont in St st, work even for 1 (3)
rows. Cont in St st, rep dec row for next row and every 4th (6th) row until 13 sts rem.
Work even in St st until back panel fits along side panels to beg of g st edging.
Change to size 3 needles and work 5 rows in k1, p1 rib. Bind off in rib.

BRIM

With RS facing and using size 3 needles and A, pick up the 67 (73) sts along cast-on edge of Bonnet. Change to B.
1st row (WS) K.
2nd row K3, *yo, k2, rep from * to end. 99 (108) sts.
3rd row K.
4th row K3, *yo, k3, rep from * to end. 131 (143) sts.
5th row K.
6th row K4, *yo, k4, rep from * to last 3 sts, yo, k3.
7th row K. Bind off.

FINISHING

Sew back panel to sides. Tie a bow at one end of each of 2 pieces of ribbon and sew bows to bonnet as shown.

MUFF

TO MAKE

Using size 6 needles and B, cast on 38 (42) sts. K one row.
2nd row K4, yarn to front between needles—called yft—, sl 1 purlwise, yarn to back between needles—called ybk—, k to last 5 sts, yft, sl 1 purlwise, ybk, k4.
Rep last 2 rows until Muff measures 9½ (10¼)″. Bind off.

FINISHING

Fold back sides along slipped sts. Slip padding and lining under hems and sew in place. Join muff seam and sew tog ends of lining. Tie a bow at each end of length of ribbon and sew to Muff.

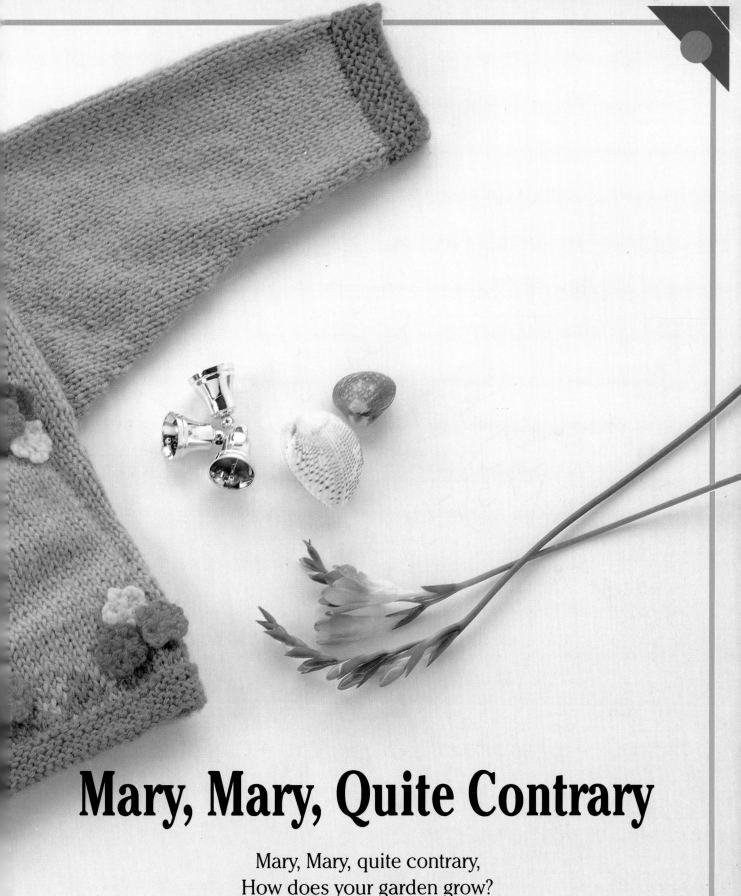

Mary, Mary, Quite Contrary

Mary, Mary, quite contrary,
How does your garden grow?
With silver bells and cockle shells
And pretty maids all in row.

MATERIALS

Sunbeam *Pure New Wool* or other sport yarn:

7 (8¾, 8¾)oz in Blue (A)
1¾oz each in Green (B), Pale Pink (C), Bright Pink (D), Dark Pink (E), and Black (F)
6 buttons
Ribbon for necklace and doll
Stuffing and scraps of felt for doll
Remnant of floral fabric and lace for doll
One pair each of sizes 3, 5, and 6 needles *or size to obtain correct gauge*
Size D crochet hook

MEASUREMENTS

To fit approx 2 (4, 6) years
Finished chest measurement 24¾ (27, 29¼)″
Length 11 (13, 15)″
Sleeve seam 9 (10½, 12)″

GAUGE

24 sts and 30 rows to 4″ over St st using size 6 needles
To save time, take time to check gauge.

ABBREVIATIONS

See page 10 for abbreviations.

CARDIGAN

POCKET LINING

Using size 6 needles and A, cast on 22 (24, 26) sts. Beg with a k row and working k1 at each end of p rows, work 24 rows in St st. Break off yarn and leave sts on a st holder.

FRONT AND BACK

Front and Back are worked tog to armholes.
Using size 3 needles and B, cast on 141 (155, 169) sts and k 7 rows.
Break off yarn and using A, k one row.
Change to size 6 needles and beg with a k row, work in St st foll rows 1-6 of chart, so ending with a p row.
Cont with A only in St st until piece measures 5¾ (7¼, 8¾)″ from beg, ending with a p row.

Right Front
Next row K35 (38, 42), turn leaving

rem sts on a spare needle.
Cont on these sts only in St st, work one row. Dec one st at beg of next row (front edge), then dec one st at front edge on every foll 3rd row until 24 (28, 30) sts rem. Work even until Right Front measures 5¼ (5¾, 6¼)″ from beg of armhole slit, ending at armhole edge.
Bind off 8 (9, 10) sts at armhole edge twice. Work one row and bind off rem 8 (10, 10) sts.

Back
With RS facing, rejoin A to sts on spare needle and k next 71 (79, 85) sts, turn. Cont on these center sts until Back measures same as Front to shoulder, ending with a p row.
Bind off 8 (9, 10) sts at beg of next 4 rows, then 8 (10, 10) sts at beg of next 2 rows. Bind off rem 23 (23, 25) sts for back neck.

Left Front
With right side facing, rejoin A to rem sts and k8 (8, 9) sts, slip next 22 (24, 26) sts onto a st holder, k across pocket lining sts, k to end.
Complete as for Right Front, reversing shaping.

SLEEVES

Using size 3 needles and B, cast on 35 (37, 39) sts. Work 9 rows in g st.
Break off B and using A, k one row. P next row, inc 6 (8, 8) sts evenly across row. 41 (45, 47) sts.
Change to size 6 needles and cont in St st, inc one st at each end of 9th row, then at each end of every foll 6th row until there are 47 (53, 59) sts, then at each end of every foll 4th row until there are 63 (69, 75) sts.
Work even in St st until Sleeve measures 9 (10½, 12)″ from beg.
Bind off.
Make 2nd Sleeve in same way.

POCKET TOP

With RS facing and using size 3 needles and B, k pocket sts from st holder. Work 6 rows in g st.
Bind off loosely.

FRONT BANDS

Join shoulder seams.

Cardigan chart

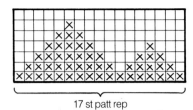

17 st patt rep

KEY

☐ = A
☒ = B

Using size 3 needles and B, cast on 7 sts. Work in g st until Band, when slightly stretched, fits up Left Front to center back of neck.
Bind off. Sew Band to Left Front.
Mark positions on Band for 6 buttons evenly spaced, the first ½″ from lower edge and the last at beg of neck shaping.
1st row K3, bind off 2 sts, k to end.
2nd row K, casting on 2 sts over those bound off.

FLOWERS

Using crochet hook and C, ch 3 and join in a ring with a sl st, [ch 4 and sl st firmly in ring] 5 times. Fasten off.
Make 10 flowers each in C, D, and E for cardigan. Make 5 each in D and E for necklace.

FINISHING

Sew pocket lining to WS and top to RS. Join sleeve seams and set into armholes. Sew on Buttonhole Band and join center back seam. Sew on flowers in groups of 3 as shown, placing one group on pocket, 4 across lower edge of Fronts and 5 across Back. Sew on buttons. For necklace thread flowers onto a length of ribbon.

DOLL

FRONT AND BACK

Using size 5 needles and C, cast on 12 sts for legs. Work in St st for 2½″, ending with a p row. Cont in St st throughout, cast on 8 sts at beg of next 2 rows for arms. Work even for ¾″, ending with a p row. Bind off 8

sts at beg of next 2 rows to complete arms.
Dec one st at each end of next 2 rows, then inc one st at each end of every other row until there are 16 sts. Work even for ¾". Dec one st at each end of every row until 8 sts

rem. Bind off.
Make 2nd piece in same way.

FINISHING
With RS of both pieces facing, sew around outer edge, leaving lower edge open. Stuff toy, and then sew

tog opening. Complete by working backstitch through all thicknesses for 1½" to denote legs. Cut felt pieces for features on face, add strands of F for hair and complete by making a simple dress from fabric and trim with lace.

Ten Little Indians

Ten Little Indians standing in a line,
One toddled home and then there were nine.
Nine little Indians swinging on a gate,
One tumbled off and then there were eight.

Fringed Patterned Jacket and Legwarmers

Fringed Patterned Jacket and Legwarmers

MATERIALS

Sirdar *Country Style DK* or other sport yarn:
5¼ (7, 8¾)oz in Mustard (A)
3½ (3½, 5¼)oz in Tan (B)
1¾oz each in Red (C), Brown (D), and Jade (E)
5 buttons
One pair each of sizes 3 and 6 needles *or size to obtain correct gauge*
Size D crochet hook

MEASUREMENTS

To fit approx 2 (4, 6) years
Finished chest measurement 25½ (27½, 29½)"
Length 15½ (17, 18½)"
Sleeve seam 10¼ (12¼, 14¼)"

GAUGE

24 sts and 30 rows to 4" over pat using size 6 needles
To save time, take time to check gauge.

ABBREVIATIONS

See page 10 for abbreviations.

JACKET

BACK

Using size 3 needles and B, cast on 73 (79, 85) sts. Work 1½ (2, 2)" in k1, p1 rib, ending with a WS row and inc 4 sts evenly across last row. 77 (83, 89) sts.
Break off B.
Change to size 6 needles and beg with a k row, working in St st foll chart, reading right to left for k rows and left to right for p rows, beg at T (S, R) work the 4 (7, 10) end sts, then rep pat sts from U to V to last 1 (4, 7) sts and work to W (X, Y).
Cont in this way, foll chart and working between T (S, R) and W (X, Y) until 66th chart row has been completed.
67th-75th rows Using A, cont in St st.
76th row (WS) Using A, k to form p ridge on RS for fringe.
77th-80th rows Using A, and beg with a k row, work in St st.
**Beg with chart row 81, cont foll chart until 90th (100th, 100th) row has been completed.

For 3rd size only: rep chart rows 25-38 using B in place of E.
For all sizes: cont with A only and work even in St st until Back measures 15½ (17, 18½)" from beg, ending with a WS row.**

Shoulder Shaping
Bind off 9 (10, 10) sts at beg of next 4 rows and 9 (8, 10) sts at beg of foll 2 rows. Bind off rem 23 (27, 29) sts for back neck.

LEFT FRONT

Using size 3 needles and B, cast on 44 (47, 50) sts.
Work 1½ (2, 2)" in k1, p1 rib, ending with a RS row.
Next row Rib across first 9 sts and slip them onto a holder, then rib to end, inc 2 sts evenly across row. 37 (40, 43) sts.
Break off B.
Change to size 6 needles and work from chart as for Back, but working between T (S, R) and Z until 66th chart row has been completed.

Neck Shaping
67th-75th rows Using A, cont in St st for 9 rows, dec one st at neck edge on 3rd, 6th and 9th rows of these 9 rows.
76th row As 76th row for Back.
77th-80th rows Using A and beg with a k row, work 4 rows in St st, dec one st at neck edge on the 2nd of these 4 rows. 33 (36, 39) sts.
Work as for Back from ** to ** *and at the same time* dec one st at neck on next row and then on every foll 3rd (3rd, 4th) row until there are 27 (28, 30) sts, then cont even until Front measures same as Back to shoulder, ending at armhole edge.

Shoulder Shaping
Bind off 9 (10, 10) sts at armhole edge twice.
Work one row. Bind off rem 9 (8, 10) sts.

RIGHT FRONT

Using size 3 needles and B, cast on 44 (47, 50) sts. Work ½" in k1, p1 rib, ending with a WS row.
Work buttonhole as foll:
1st buttonhole row (RS) Rib 3,

bind off 3 sts, rib to end.
2nd buttonhole row Work in rib, casting on 3 sts over those bound off.
Cont in rib until ribbing measures 1½ (2, 2)", ending with a RS row.
Next row *Rib 35 (38, 41) inc 2 sts evenly across these sts, slip rem 9 sts onto a st holder. 37 (40, 43) sts.
Break off B.
Change to size 6 needles and work from chart as for Back, but working between U and W (X, Y), and complete as for Right Front, reversing shaping.

SLEEVES

Using size 3 needles and B, cast on 40 sts, Work 1½ (2, 2)" in k1, p1 rib, ending with a row WS and inc 7 sts evenly across last row. 47 sts.
Break off B.
Change to size 6 needles and work from chart as for Back, but working between S and X to beg *and at the same time* inc one st at each end of 7th row and then every foll 6th row until 66th chart row has been completed, working incs into pat. 67 sts.
For first size only: Bind off.
For 2nd and 3rd sizes: Working in St st throughout, cont to inc one st at each end of every 6th row until there are 71 (77) sts and then work even *and at the same time* work 4 rows in A only and then foll chart from chart row 81 until 86th (102nd) chart rows have been completed. Bind off.
Make 2nd Sleeve in same way.

FINISHING

Join shoulder seams.

Button Band and Collar
Using size 3 needles, rejoin B to inside edge of 9 sts of Left Front.
Cont in rib until Band fits up front edge to first neck dec.
Mark the positions of 5 equally spaced buttons along Band, the first to correspond with buttonhole already made and the last at first neck dec. Then cont in rib, inc one st at inner edge on next row and then every other row until there are 25 (29, 31) sts.

76

Work even in rib until shaped edge of Collar fits up left front neck edge to center back neck. Bind off in rib.

Buttonhole Band and Collar
Work as for Button Band and Collar, but making 4 more buttonholes to correspond with button positions. Sew shaped edges of Bands and Collar to jacket, then join center back seam. Placing center of Sleeve at shoulder seam, sew bound-off edge of Sleeves to top part of Back and Fronts. Join side and sleeve seams.

For fringe, knot two 4½" lengths of D folded double through every other st of p ridges. Mark center st of Sleeves. Knot two 4½" lengths of D folded double through center st on every 3rd row of Sleeves. Trim fringe and sew on buttons.

LEGWARMERS

TO MAKE

Using size 3 needles and B, cast on 47 (47, 53) sts and work 2½ (3, 3½)" in k1, p1 rib, ending with a WS row. Break off B.

Change to size 6 needles and work from chart as for Back, but working between S (S, R) and X (X, Y) until 66th row has been completed.

Using A, only work 4 rows more in St st. Break off A.

Change to size 3 needles and using B, work 2½ (3, 3½)" in k1, p1 rib. Bind off in rib.

Make 2nd Legwarmer in same way. Join seams.

Chart for jacket, sleeves, and legwarmers

For SLEEVE, continue chart exactly as it appears, omitting extra St st rows.

For JACKET St st rows 67-75; purl row 76; St st rows 77-80

KEY
☐ = A
⊡ = B
⊠ = C
⬤ = D
⧄ = E

Z Y X W V   12 pat sts   U T S R

77

Jack Frost

Look out, look out,
Jack Frost is about.
He'll wipe your fingers and bite your toes,
And leave red noses wherever he goes.

Child's Snowflake Sweater, Earmuff, and Scarf

Child's Snowflake Sweater, Earmuff and Scarf

MATERIALS
Copley *Sonata DK* or other sport yarn:
10½ (10½, 14)oz in Burgundy (A)
3½oz in White (B)
Burgundy hairband for earmuff
One pair each of sizes 3 and 6 needles *or size to obtain correct gauge*
Size 3 circular needle

MEASUREMENTS
To fit approx 2 (4, 6) years
Finished chest measurement 25¾ (28, 30¼)"
Length 13 (14¼, 15¾)"
Sleeve seam 11¼ (12¼, 13¾)"

GAUGE
22 sts and 30 rows to 4" over St st using size 6 needles
To save time, take time to check gauge.

ABBREVIATIONS
See page 10 for abbreviations.

SWEATER

BACK
Using size 3 needles and A, cast on 66 (70, 74) sts.
1st row rib (RS) K2, *p2, k2, rep from * to end.
2nd row rib P2, *k2, p2, rep from * to end.
Rep these 2 rib rows until ribbing measures 1½ (2, 2)", ending with a first rib row.
Next row (WS) Rib 9 (5, 5) sts, *work into front and back of next st —called inc 1—, rib 11 (9, 7), rep from * to last 9 (5, 5) sts, inc 1, rib to end. 71 (77, 83) sts.
Change to size 6 needles and beg with a k row, work in St st foll chart beg and ending as indicated for chosen size until 48 (50, 56) rows of chart have been completed, so ending with a WS row.

Armhole Shaping
Cont to foll chart as set, bind off 6 (7, 7) sts at beg of next 2 rows. 59 (63, 69) sts.**
Work even foll chart until 86 (92, 104) rows of chart have been completed.

Shoulder Shaping
Cont in St st, bind off 15 (16, 17) sts at beg of next 2 rows. Slip rem 29 (31, 35) sts onto a st holder for back neck.

FRONT
Work as for Back to **.
Work even foll chart until 62 (66, 74) rows of chart have been completed.

Neck Shaping
Cont foll chart *and at the same time* work neck shaping as foll:
Next row (RS) K15 (16, 17), turn leaving rem sts on a spare needle. Cont on these sts only, work even foll chart until Front measures same as Back to shoulder. Bind off. Return to rem sts and with RS facing, slip 29 (31, 35) sts at center front onto a st holder, then rejoin yarn at neck edge of rem set of 15 (16, 17) sts and work in pat to end. Work even foll chart until Front measures same as Back to shoulder. Bind off.

SLEEVES
Using size 3 needles and A, cast on 30 (30, 34) sts and work 1¼" in k2, p2 rib as for Back, ending with a first rib row.
Next row (WS) Rib 2 (2, 4) sts, *inc 1, rib 2 (1, 1), rep from * to last 1 (2, 4) sts, inc 1, rib to end. 40 (44, 48) sts.
Change to size 6 needles and beg with a k row, work in St st foll chart beg and ending as indicated for chosen size, and inc one st at each end of 7th row and then every foll 6th row until there are 56 (62, 70) sts. Then work even foll chart until row 82 (92, 104) has been completed. Bind off.
Make 2nd Sleeve in same way.

COLLAR
Join shoulder seams.
With RS facing and size 3 circular needle and A, k29 (31, 35) sts from st holder at center front, pick up and k22 (24, 27) sts evenly up right front neck edge, k29 (31, 35) sts from st holder at center back inc one st at center back, and pick up and k22 (24, 27) sts down left front edge. 103 (111, 125) sts.
Working backward and forward on circular needle in rows, work rib as foll:
1st rib row (RS) K1, *p1, k1, rep from * to end.
2nd rib row Bind off one st, work in rib to last st, inc 1.
3rd rib row Rib to end.
Rep 2nd and 3rd rib rows until Collar measures 2½ (3, 3½)" from beg, ending with a 3rd rib row.
Cont inc one st at end of next row and then every other row as set *and at the same time* bind off at beg of next and every other row 2 sts 4 times, 3 sts twice, 4 sts once, and 5 sts once, ending with a 3rd rib row.

Bind off rem 88 (96, 110) sts.

FINISHING
Sew bound-off edges of Sleeves to inner armhole edges and row ends of last 9 (10, 10) rows of Sleeves to bound-off sts at underarm. Sew side and sleeve seams. Place inc edge of left collar behind right collar and stitch along pick-up row at center front. Fold collar to RS.

EARMUFF

TO MAKE
Make 2 pompons with A and glue firmly to the ends of hairband.

SCARF

TO MAKE
Using size 3 needles and A, cast on 33 sts, work 5 rows in g st. Change to size 6 needles and beg with a k row, work 6 rows in St st, so ending with a p row.
**Next row K7A, work 19 sts of row 1 of chart, k7A.
Next row P7A, work 19 sts of row 2 of chart, p7A.
Cont in this way, work rows 3-21 of chart, so ending with a k row. Break off B.**
Using A only and beg with a p row, work 11 rows in St st, so ending with a p row.
Place a marker at each end of last row to mark position of folding line. Beg and ending with a p row, work 37 rows in St st.
Next row (RS) K.
Next row K2, p29, k2.
Rep the last 2 rows until Scarf measures 36 (39, 42)″ from markers, ending with a p row. Beg with a k row, work 38 rows in St st, omitting k2 borders on WS and so ending with a p row.
Place a marker at each end of last row to mark position of folding line. Beg with a p row, work 11 rows in St st, so ending with a p row.
Rep from ** to ** once. Using A only and beg with a p row, work 6 rows in St st, so ending with a k row. Change to size 3 needles and work 5 rows in g st. Bind off.

FINISHING
Fold each end of scarf to RS along folding line at markers and sew along side edges to form pockets.

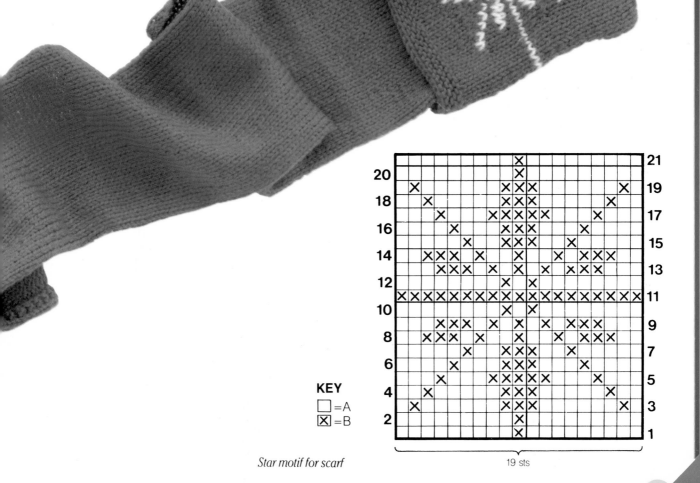

KEY
□ = A
⊠ = B

Star motif for scarf　　19 sts

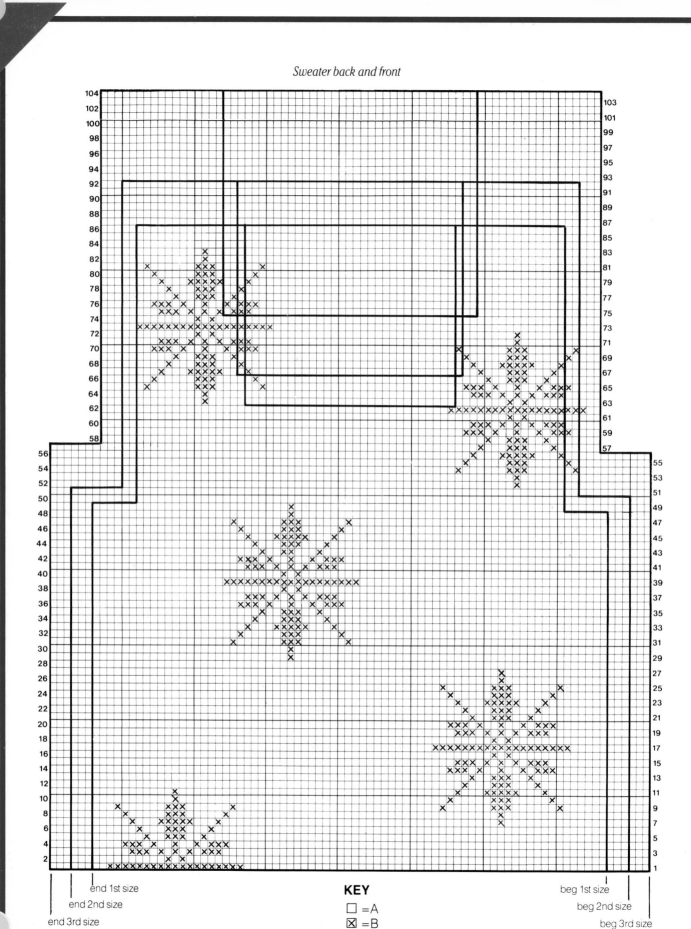

Sweater back and front

KEY

☐ = A
☒ = B

Sweater sleeve

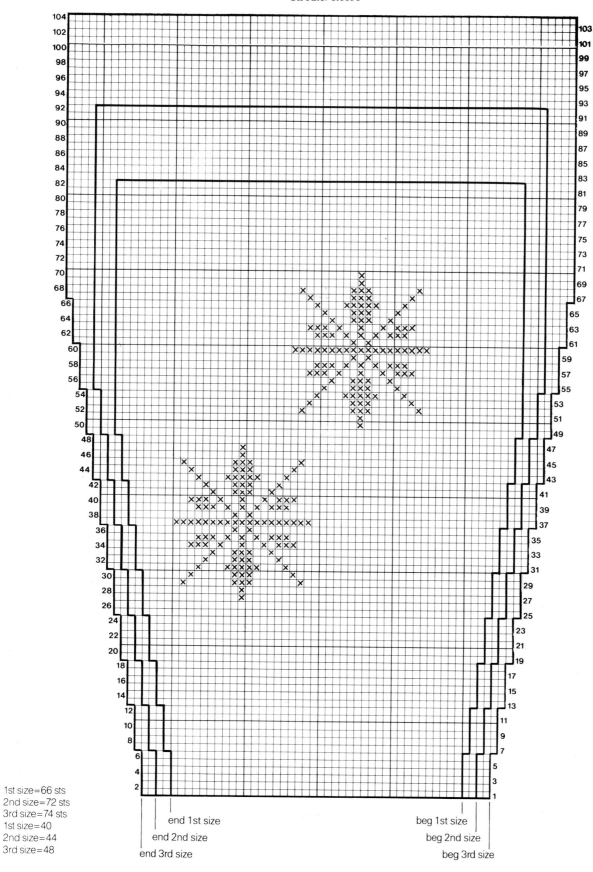

1st size=66 sts
2nd size=72 sts
3rd size=74 sts
1st size=40
2nd size=44
3rd size=48

end 1st size
end 2nd size
end 3rd size

beg 1st size
beg 2nd size
beg 3rd size

Twinkle, Twinkle Little Star

Twinkle, twinkle little star,
How I wonder what you are!
Up above the world so high
Like a diamond in the sky!

Star Dress,
Bolero, and Purse

Star Dress, Bolero, and Purse

MATERIALS

Dress and purse

Spectrum *Detroit DK* or other sport yarn:

7 (10½, 14)oz in Blue (A)

3½oz in Yellow (B)

1¾oz each in Dark Blue (C), Red (D), Light Blue (E), and White (F)

Spectrum *Vermont 4 ply* or other fingering yarn for collar:

1oz in White (G)

5 white buttons

One pair each of sizes 3, 6, and 9 needles *or size to obtain correct gauge*

Size F crochet hook

Bolero

Spectrum *Pirouette* or other mohair yarn:

5 (6, 7)oz in Blue (H)

One pair of size 7 needles *or size to obtain correct gauge*

Size G crochet hook

MEASUREMENTS

To fit approx 2 (4, 6) years

Finished dress chest measurement at armhole 24 (24¾, 25½)″

Dress length 23½ (24½, 25½″)

Dress sleeve seam 9½ (10½, 11½)″

Finished bolero chest measurement 26 (28, 30)″

Bolero length 12½ (13½, 15)″

Bolero sleeve seam 7 (7½, 8)″

GAUGE

Dress

22 sts and 30 rows to 4″ over St st using size 6 needles and A

Bolero

16 sts and 20 rows to 4″ over St st using size 7 needles and H

To save time, take time to check gauge.

ABBREVIATIONS

See page 10 for abbreviations.

DRESS

BACK

Using size 3 needles and A, cast on 118 (122, 126) sts.

Beg with a k row, work 2 rows in St st. Change to size 6 needles and cont in St st *and at the same time* place star motifs as foll:

9th row (RS) K22, work chart row 1

Star motif

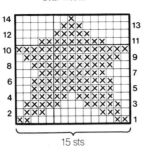

15 sts

of star motif in C over next 15 sts, k to end.

37th row K to last 56 sts, work star motif in D over next 15 sts, k to end.

53rd row K32, work star motif in E over next 15 sts k to end.

73rd row K to last 36 sts, work star motif in B over next 15 sts, k to end.

91st row K45, work star motif in C over next 15 sts, k to end.

After the motifs have been completed, work even in St st until Skirt measures 19½ (20, 20½)″ from beg, ending with a WS row.

Yoke Shaping

Next row K7, *k2tog, rep from * to last 7 sts, k7. 66 (68, 70) sts.

Beg with a p row, work 3 rows in St st, so ending with a WS row.**

Armhole Shaping

1st row Bind off 2 sts, k until there are 31 (32, 33) sts on left-hand needle, turn leaving rem sts on a spare needle.

2nd row P into front and back of first st, p to end.

3rd row Bind off 2 sts, k9, work star motif in D over next 15 sts, k to end.

4th row P.

5th row As 3rd row.

P one row. Cont in St st throughout, dec one st at beg of next and every other row 2 times in all. 26 (27, 28) sts. When motif has been completed, work even until piece measures 4 (4½, 5)″ from Skirt dec row, ending with a WS row.

Shoulder Shaping

Bind off 5 sts at beg of next row, then 4 sts at beg of foll 2 RS rows. Leave rem 13 (14, 15) sts on a st holder.

Rejoin yarn to rem sts and complete to match first side reversing shaping, but after last armhole dec row (RS) has been worked, work 3 rows, then place star motif on next row as foll:

Next row K to last 20 sts, work star motif in E over next 15 sts, k to end.

FRONT

Work as for Back to **.

Armhole Shaping

Bind off 2 sts at beg of next 6 rows, then dec one st at each end of next and every other row 2 times in all *and at the same time* place star motif in D as for Back, so ending with a RS row. 50 (52, 54) sts. Work 3 rows.

Place star motif in E on next row as for Back and work even until Front is 8 (8, 10) rows less than Back to shoulder, ending with a WS row.

Neck Shaping

Next row K20, turn leaving rem sts on a spare needle.

Cont on these sts only for first side, dec one st at neck edge on next 7 rows. Work even for 1 (1, 3) rows. 13 sts.

Shoulder Shaping

Bind off 5 sts at beg of next row, then 4 sts at beg of every other row 2 times.

Return to rem sts and with RS facing, slip center 10 (12, 14) sts onto a st holder, then rejoin yarn and k to end. Complete to match first side, reversing shaping.

SLEEVES

Using size 3 needles and F, cast on 38 (40, 42) sts. Work 1½″ in k1, p1 rib. Break off F.

Change to size 6 needles and using A, k one row, inc one st at each end of row. 40 (42, 44) sts.

Beg with a p row and cont in St st throughout, inc one st at each end of every 10th row until there are 44 (46, 50) sts *and at the same time* place star motifs as foll:

3rd row K4, work star motif in D over next 15 sts, k to end.

19th row K to last 22 sts, work star motif in E over next 15 sts, k to end.
33rd row K13, work star motif in B over next 15 sts, k to end.
47th row K27, work star motif in C over next 15 sts, k to end.
Work even until Sleeve measures 9½ (10½, 11½)″ from beg, ending with a WS row.

Cap Shaping
Bind off 2 sts at beg of next 6 rows, then dec one st at each end of next row and every other row until there are 22 (24, 26) sts, so ending with a RS row.
P one row.
Bind off 2 sts at beg of next 2 rows and 2 (3, 4) sts at beg of foll 2 rows.
Bind off rem 14 sts.
Make 2nd Sleeve in same way.

NECKBAND
Join shoulder seams. With RS facing and using size 3 needles and A, k13 (14, 15) sts from left back neck st holder, pick up and k13 sts down left front neck, k10 (12, 14) sts from center front neck st holder, pick up and k13 sts up right front neck, and k13 (14, 15) from right back neck st holder. 62 (66, 70) sts.
Break off A. Using F, p one row, then work 5 rows in k1, p1 rib.
Bind off sts in rib.

BACK BANDS
With RS facing and using size 3 needles and F, pick up and k30 sts evenly along back opening from top of neckband to lower edge of opening.
Work 2 rows in k1, p1 rib.
Next row (buttonhole row) Rib 2, *yo, k2tog, rib 6, rep from * to last 4 sts, yo, k2tog, rib 2.
Work 2 rows in rib. Bind off in rib.
Work rem Band in same way on other side of opening, beg at lower edge of opening and omitting buttonholes.

FINISHING
Join side and sleeve seams. Sew in sleeves. Sew on buttons. Using size F crochet hook and A, work 2 rows of sc along lower edge of Skirt.
Work shooting star lines in backstitch as shown.

DETACHABLE COLLAR
Using size F crochet hook and G, ch7.
Base row 1dc in 4th ch from hook, 1dc in each ch to end. Turn. 5 sts.
1st row Ch3 to count as first dc, skip first dc, 1dc in next dc, ch2, skip next 2dc, 1dc in 3rd of ch-3, *yo and insert hook in base loop of last dc worked, yo and draw a loop through, yo and draw a loop through first loop on hook, [yo and draw through 2 loops on hook] twice*, rep from * to * twice more. Turn at end of each row.
2nd row Ch5, 1dc in 4th ch from hook, 1dc in next ch, 1dc in next dc, ch2, skip next 2dc, 1dc in next dc, 2dc in ch-2 sp, 1dc in next dc, 1dc in 3rd of ch-3.
3rd row Ch3, skip first dc, 1dc in next dc, ch2, skip next 2dc, 1dc in next dc, 2dc in ch-2 sp, 1dc in next dc, ch2, skip next 2dc, 1dc in 3rd of ch-3, rep from * to * of first row 3 times.
4th row 1sl st in each of first 4dc, ch3 to count as first dc, 2dc in ch-2 sp, 1dc in next dc, ch2, skip next 2dc, 1dc in next dc, 2dc in ch-2 sp, 1dc in next dc, 1dc in 3rd of ch-3.
5th row Ch3, skip first dc, 1dc in next dc, ch2, skip next 2dc, 1dc in next dc, 2dc in ch-2 sp, 1dc in next dc.
6th row 1sl st in each of first 4dc, ch3 to count as first dc, 2dc in ch-2 sp, 1dc in next dc, 1dc in 3rd of ch-3.
First-6th rows form each basic motif. Rep first-6th rows 6 times more, so ending with a 6th row, do not turn.
Working along straight edge of Collar, work one row of dc to end of straight edge, do not turn. Sl st along foundation ch to first corner (5th foundation ch), *[ch3, sl st in next corner] 3 times, sl st to corner edge of same dc, [ch3, sl st to next corner] twice, ch3, sl st to next corner on next motif, rep from * to end, omitting last sl st to next corner and instead sl st in next corner on same motif then sl st along to within border row, ch2, sl st in top of first dc of border to form buttonhole loop. Fasten off.
Sew on button. Collar can be basted in place.

BOLERO
BACK AND FRONT
Using size 7 needles and H, cast on 52 (56, 60) sts. Work in St st until Back measures 7 (7½, 8½)″ from beg. Mark both ends of last row for armhole. Work 5 (5½, 6)″ more in St st, ending with a WS row.

Back Neck Shaping
Next row K17 (18, 19) sts, bind off center 18 (20, 22) sts, k to end. Cont on these last 17 (18, 19) sts only, p one row and slip other side onto a spare needle. Mark both ends of last row for shoulder.

Front Neck Shaping
Cont in St st throughout, inc one st at beg of next row and at same edge on next 3 rows. Cast on 5 (6, 7) sts at beg of next row. 26 (28, 30) sts. Work even until armhole is same length as back armhole between markers. Mark side edge of last row as end of armhole, then work even until Left Front is 8 rows less than Back to cast-on edge, ending with a WS row. Dec one st at beg of next row and at same edge on foll 7 rows. Bind off rem 18 (20, 22) sts. Complete Right Front to match Left Front, reversing shaping.

SLEEVES
With RS facing and using size 7 needles and H, pick up and k44 (48, 52) sts betweem armhole markers. Beg with a p row, work 7 (7½, 8½)″ in St st. Bind off.

FINISHING
Join side and sleeve seams. Using size G crochet hook and H, work 2 rows of sc around sleeve edges, and around lower edges, fronts and neck, working 3 sc in each neck corner.

PURSE
TO MAKE
Using size 9 needles and B double throughout, cast on 25 sts. Work in g st (k every row) for 8″. Bind off. Work a 2nd piece in same way. Sew three sides of purse. Using size 9 needles and A, cast on 86 sts, then bind off. Thread cord through Purse 7 rows from top to finish.

Pussy Cat, Pussy Cat

Pussy cat, pussy cat, where have you been?
I've been to London to visit the Queen.
Pussy cat, pussy cat, what did you there?
I frightened a little mouse under her chair.

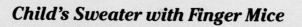

Child's Sweater with Finger Mice

MATERIALS
Emu *Superwash DK* or other sport yarn:
7 (8¾, 10½)oz in Yellow (A)
1¾ (1¾, 3½)oz in Black (B)
1¼oz in Gray (C)
Small amount in White (E)
Emu *Kid Mohair* or other mohair yarn:
1¾oz in Black (D)
Small amount of white felt

One pair each of sizes 3 and 6 needles *or size to obtain correct gauge*
Size D crochet hook

MEASUREMENTS
To fit approx 2 (4, 6) years
Finished chest measurement 24 (26¼, 29)"
Length 14 (15, 16)"

Sleeve seam 8½ (9½, 10½)"

GAUGE
22 sts and 27 rows to 4" over pat using size 6 needles
To save time, take time to check gauge.

ABBREVIATIONS
See page 10 for abbreviations.

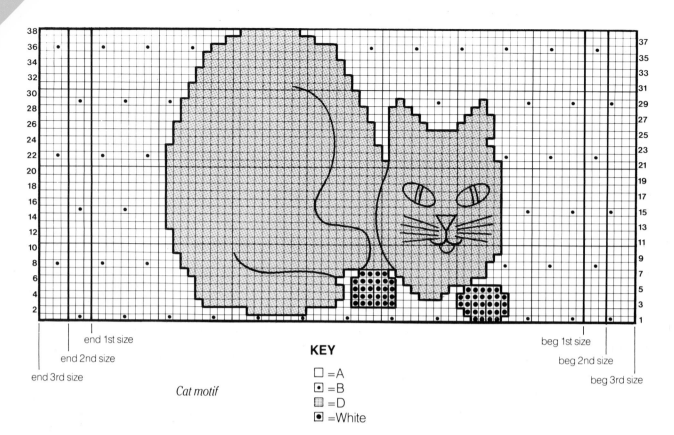

KEY

☐ = A
☑ = B
▦ = D
◉ = White

Cat motif

SWEATER

BACK

Using size 3 needles and A, cast on 65 (71, 79) sts.

1st rib row (RS) K1, *p1, k1 rep from * to end.

2nd rib row P1, *k1, p1, rep from * to end.

Rep these 2 rib rows for 2", ending with a 2nd row and inc one st at center of last row. 66 (72, 80) sts. Change to size 6 needles and work in pat as foll:

1st row (RS) K with A.

2nd row P with A.**

3rd row K1(4, 2)A, *1B, 5A, rep from * to last 5 (2, 6) sts, 1B, 4 (1, 5)A.

4th row As 2nd row.

5th-8th rows Rep first and 2nd rows twice.

9th row As first row.

10th row P2 (4, 2)A, *1B, 5A, rep from * to last 5 (2, 6) sts, 1B, 4 (1, 5)A.

11th-14th rows As 5th-8th rows. These 14 rows form the pat rep. Cont in pat until Back measures 14 (15, 16)" from beg, ending with a WS row.
Bind off.

FRONT

Work as for Back to **.

Cont in St st foll chart from row 1, reading odd-numbered (k) rows from right to left and even (p) rows from left to right, using a separate small ball of yarn for each area of color and twisting colors tog at back of work when changing colors to avoid making holes, until 38th chart row has been completed. Break off D.

Cont in pat as for Back, beg with the 13th pat row, until Front measures 12½ (13½, 14½)" from beg, ending with a WS row.

Neck Shaping

Next row Work 26 (29, 33) sts in pat, k2tog, turn leaving rem sts on a spare needle.

Cont in pat on these 27 (30, 34) sts only, dec one st at neck edge on every row until 21 (23, 26) sts rem. Work even until Front measures same as Back to shoulder, ending with a WS row. Bind off.

Return to rem sts on spare needle and with RS facing, rejoin yarn and bind off first 10 sts, work in pat to end of row. Complete to match first side of neck, reversing shaping.

SLEEVES

Using size 3 needles and B, cast on 37 (41, 45) sts. Work 1½" in rib as for Back, ending with a RS row.

Next row Rib 2 (1, 8), *insert tip of left-hand needle under horizontal strand before next st and work into back of it—called m1—, rib 3 (3, 2), rep from * to last 2 (1, 7)sts, m1, rib to end. 49 (55, 61)sts.

Change to size 6 needles and work in pat as foll:

1st row K with A.

2nd row P with A.

3rd row K3A, *1B, 5A, rep from * to last 4 sts, 1B, 3A.

4th row P with A.

5th-8th rows Rep first and 2nd rows twice.

9th row K with A.

10th row P1B, *5A, 1B, rep from * to end.

11th-14th rows As 5th-8th rows. These 14 rows form the pat rep. Cont in pat until Sleeve measures 8½ (9½, 10½)" from beg, ending with a WS row. Bind off loosely. Make 2nd Sleeve in same way.

SLEEVE POCKETS

Using size 6 needles and B, cast on 16 sts.

1st row K with B.
2nd row P with B.
Using a separate length of yarn for each section and twisting yarns tog at back of work when changing colors to avoid holes, cont as foll:
3rd row [K2B, 5A] twice, 2B.
4th row [P2B, 5A] twice, 2B.
5th-10th rows Rep 3rd and 4th rows 3 times.
11th row As 3rd row.
12th row P with B.
13th row K with B.
14th row As 4th row.
15th-20th rows Rep 3rd and 4th rows 3 times.
21st row As 13th row.
22nd row As 12th row.
Bind off in B.
Make 2nd Pocket in same way.

NECKBAND

Join right shoulder seam. Place a marker on bound-off edge of Back 21 (23, 26) sts from armhole edge to denote beg of left shoulder. With RS facing and using size 3 needles and B, pick up and k16 (17, 18) sts down left front neck, 10 sts across center front neck, 16 (17, 18) sts up right front neck, then 25 (27, 29) sts to marker. 67 (71, 75) sts.
Work 5 rows in k1, p1 rib as for Back. Bind off in rib.

COLLAR

Using size 3 needles and B, cast on 69 (71, 73) sts and work 5 rows in rib as for Back. Change to size 6 needles and cont in rib until Collar measures 2½". Bind off in rib.

MICE

Using size D crochet hook and C, ch11 and join with a sc to first ch to form a ring. Work in continuous rounds of sc on these 11sc until mouse measures approx 2½".
Dec 3 sts evenly across each of next 3 rounds. 2sc. Fasten off.
Using B, ch3 and join with a sl st to first chain. Join to top of head for ear. Work 2nd ear in same way.
Embroider eyes and nose in B.
Make 5 more mice in same way.

FINISHING

Join left shoulder and neckband seam. Sew Collar to pick up row of neckband on WS. Fold Sleeves in half lengthwise. Place fold at shoulder seams and sew in position. Join side and sleeve seams. Sew pockets to sleeves. Put mice in pockets.
Using felt, cut out eyes, mouth, and nose shapes for cat and sew to face. Using C embroider lines in chain st on cat, and using B work paw details as shown on chart. Using B work a line across eyes, and using E work whiskers.

Ladybird, Ladybird

Ladybird, ladybird,
Fly away home,
Your house is on fire,
And your children all gone.

Child's Coat, Hat, and Mittens

MATERIALS

Emu *Snowstorm Tweed* or other bulky yarn for coat:
21 (24½, 28)oz in Red Tweed (A)
Emu *Superwash DK* or other sport yarn for hat and mittens:
1¾oz each in Red (B) and Black (C)
3 buttons
One pair each sizes 3, 6, 10½, and 11 needles *or size to obtain correct gauge*

MEASUREMENTS

To fit approx 2 (4, 6) years
Finished chest measurement 28¾ (32, 35¼)"
Length 17½ (19½, 22½)"
Sleeve seam 9 (10½, 12)"

GAUGE

10 sts and 22 rows to 4" over g st using size 11 needles and A
22 sts and 30 rows to 4" over St st using size 6 needles and B
To save time, take time to check gauge.

ABBREVIATIONS

See page 10 for abbreviations.

COAT

BACK

Using size 10½ needles and A, cast on 35 (39, 43) sts.
1st rib row (RS) K1, *p1, k1, rep from * to end.
2nd rib row P1, *k1, p1, rep from * to end.
Rep these 2 rib rows for 1", ending with a 2nd row and inc one st at center of last row. 36 (40, 44) sts.
Change to size 11 needles and work in g st (k every row) until Back measures 17½ (19½, 22½)" from beg, ending with a WS row. Bind off.

LEFT FRONT

Using size 10½ needles and A, cast on 13 (15, 17) sts and work 1" in k1, p1 rib as for Back, ending with a 2nd rib row and for 3rd size only inc one st at center of last row. 13 (15, 18) sts. Change to size 11 needles and work in g st until Front measures 15½ (18, 20½)" from beg, ending with a WS row.

Neck Shaping
Cont in g st throughout, dec one st at neck edge on next row then on every other row 1 (1, 3) times more. 11 (13, 14) sts.
Work even until Front measures same as Back to shoulder, ending with a WS row. Bind off.

RIGHT FRONT

Using size 10½ needles and A, cast on 21 (23, 27) sts and work 1" in k1, p1 rib as for Back, ending with a 2nd rib row and for 2nd size only inc one st at center of last row. 21 (24, 27) sts.
Change to size 11 needles and work in g st until Front measures 15½ (18, 20½)" from beg, ending with a WS row.

Neck Shaping
Cont in g st throughout, bind off 8 (8, 10) sts at beg of next row. Work even for one row.
Dec one st at neck edge on next row and then on every other row until 11 (13, 14) sts rem.
Work even until Right Front measures same as Left Front to shoulder. Bind off.

SLEEVES

Using size 11 needles and A, cast on 15 (17, 19) sts and work 1¼" in k1, p1 rib as for Back, ending with a first rib row.
Next row Rib 3 (1, 1), work into front and back of each st to end. 27 (33, 37) sts.
Work in g st until Sleeve measures 9 (10½, 12½)", ending with a WS row. Bind off loosely.
Make 2nd Sleeve in same way.

Spot motif

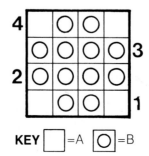

KEY ☐ =A ◯ =B

NECKBAND

Join shoulder seams. With RS facing and using size 10½ needles and A, pick up and k18 (18, 20) sts up right front neck, 15 (15, 17) sts across back neck, and 10 sts down left front neck. 43 (43, 47) sts. Beg with a 2nd rib row as for Back, work 5 rows in rib. Bind off in rib.

BUTTONHOLE BAND

With RS of Right front facing and using size 10½ needles and A, beg at cast-on edge and pick up and k55 (59, 63) sts evenly up Front to top of neckband.
Work 3 rows in k1, p1 rib as for Back.
Buttonhole Row (RS) Rib 34 (38, 42) sts, [k2tog, yo, rib 6] twice, k2tog, yo, rib 3.
Rib 3 rows more. Bind off in rib.

BUTTON BAND

Work as for Buttonhole Band, but along Left Front and omitting the buttonholes.

FINISHING

Sew on Sleeves. Join side and sleeve seams. Sew on buttons.

HAT

TO MAKE

Using size 3 needles and B, cast on 102 sts. Work 11 rows in k1, p1 rib.
Next row Rib 7, *work in front and back of next st—called inc—, rib 2, rep from * to last 8 sts, inc in next st, rib 7. 132 sts.
Change to size 6 needles and working in St st and placing motif from chart randomly throughout reading odd-numbered (k) chart rows from right to left and even-numbered (p) rows from left to right, work 18 rows, so ending with a p row. Then keeping to pat, beg shaping as foll:
1st row K2, *k2tog, k11, rep from * to end. 122 sts.
Work even for 3 rows.
5th row *K9, k3tog, rep from * to last 2 sts, k2. 102 sts.
Work even for 3 rows.
9th row *K7, k3tog, rep from * to last 2 sts, k2. 82 sts.
Work even for 3 rows.

13th row *K5, k3tog, rep from * to last 2 sts, k2. 62 sts.
Work even for 3 rows.
17th row *K3, k3tog, rep from * to last 2 sts, k2. 42 sts.
Work even for 3 rows.
21st row * K1, k3tog, rep from * to last 2 sts, k2. 22 sts.
Work even for 3 rows.
25th row K2tog to end. 11 sts.
Break off yarn leaving a long loose end. Thread loose end through rem sts, pull tightly and fasten securely.

FINISHING
Sew up seam. Using C, make a pompon and sew to top.

MITTENS
RIGHT MITTEN
Using size 3 needles and B, cast on 28 (30, 32) sts and work 1¼″ in k1, p1 rib. Change to size 6 needles, and working in St st and placing motif from chart randomly throughout, beg with a k row and work 2 rows in St st.**

Gusset Shaping
Next row K14 (15, 16) sts, k in front and back of next st—called inc—, k1, inc in next st, k11 (12, 13). 30 (32, 34) sts.
Work even for 3 rows.
Next row K14 (15, 16), inc in next st, k3, inc in next st, k11 (12, 13). 32 (34, 36) sts.
Cont to inc in this way on every 4th row until there are 36 (38, 40) sts.
Work even for 3 rows.
Next row K23 (25, 27) sts, turn, cast on 2 sts.
Next row P10 (11, 12) sts, turn, cast on 2 sts.

Thumb
***Work ¼ (½, ¾)″ St st on these 12 (13, 14) sts, ending with a p row.

Top of Thumb Shaping
Next row K0 (1, 1), [k2, k2tog] 3 times, k0 (0, 1). 9 (10, 11) sts.
Next row P.
Next row K1 (0, 1), [k2tog] to end. Break off yarn and thread through rem sts, fasten off and sew up seam. With RS facing, rejoin yarn to inner end of sts on right-hand needle, then pick up and k4 sts onto the same needle from base of thumb, k to end. 30 (32, 34) sts.
Work even for ¾ (1, 1)″.

Top of Mitten Shaping
1st row K2, [sl 1-k1-psso, k8 (9, 10), k2tog, k2] twice.
2nd row P.
3rd row K2, [sl 1-k1-psso, k6 (7, 8), k2tog, k2] twice.
4th row P.
5th row K2, (sl 1-k1-psso, k4 (5, 6), k2tog, k2] twice.
6th row P.
Bind off. Sew up seam.

LEFT MITTEN
Work as for Right Mitten to **.
Next row K11 (12, 13), inc in next st, k1, inc in next st, k14 (15, 16).
Work even for 3 rows.
Next row K11 (12, 13), inc in next st, k3, inc in next st, k to end.
Cont to inc in this way on every 4th row until there are 36 (38, 40) sts.
Work even for 3 rows.
Next row K19 (21, 23), turn, cast on 2 sts.
Next row P10 (11, 12) turn, cast on 2 sts.
Complete as for Right Mitten from *** to end.

Where, Oh Where, is my Little Dog Gone?

Oh where, oh where, is my little dog gone?
Oh where, oh where, can he be?
With his ears cut short and his tail cut long,
Oh where, oh where, is he?

Child's Jacket and Purse

MATERIALS
Spectrum *Detroit DK* or other sport yarn:
10½ (10½, 14)oz in Pink (A)
3½oz each in Black (B) and White (C)
4 buttons
One pair each of sizes 3 and 6 needles *or size to obtain correct gauge*
Size E crochet hook

MEASUREMENTS
To fit approx 2 (4, 6) years
Finished chest measurement 25½ (27½, 29½)″
Length 14 (15, 16)″
Sleeve seam 11 (12, 13)″

GAUGE
22sts and 30 rows to 4″ over St st using size 6 needles
To save time, take time to check gauge.

ABBREVIATIONS
See page 10 for abbreviations.

JACKET

BACK
Using size 3 needles and A, cast on 65 (70, 75) sts. K4 rows. Change to size 6 needles, k one row, and p one row. Place dog motifs foll chart on next row as foll:
1st row K1 (2, 3) sts in A, *k2B, k1A, k2B, k3A, k4B, k4 (5, 6)A, rep from * to end.
Cont in pat foll chart for motifs until 15 chart rows have been completed. Break off B.
Next row P in A.
Next row K in A.
Using C, p one row, inc 5 (6, 6) sts evenly across row. 70 (76, 81) sts.
Work in pat as foll:
1st row (RS) Using C, k7 (10, 7) sts, [p1, k10] to end, ending last rep k7 (10, 7) instead of k10.
2nd row Using A, p7 (10, 7) sts, [k1, p10] to end, ending last rep p7 (10, 7) sts instead of p10.
3rd row Using A, work as first row.
Rep last 2 rows 5 times more.
14th row Using B, as 2nd row.
Rep last 14 rows until Back measures 8 (8½, 9)″ from beg,

ending with a WS row. Mark both ends of last row as beg of armholes. Cont in pat as set until Back measures 6 (6½, 7)″ from armhole markers, ending with a WS row.

Shoulder Shaping
Bind off 12 (13, 14) sts at beg of next 4 rows. Bind off rem 22 (24, 25) sts for back neck.

LEFT FRONT

Using size 3 needles and A, cast on 33 (36, 39) sts. K 4 rows. Change to size 6 needles, k one row, then p one row. Place 2 dog motifs foll chart on next row as foll:
1st row K1 (2, 3) A, *k2B, k1A, k2B, k3A, k4B, k4 (5, 6)A, rep from * to end.
Cont in pat foll chart for motifs until 15 chart rows have been completed. Break off B.
Using A, p one row, k one row.
Using C, p one row, inc 4 (5, 4) sts evenly across row. 37 (41, 43) sts.
Work in pat as for Back as foll:
1st row (RS) Using C, k7 (10, 7), [p1, k10] to end, ending last rep k7 (8, 7) at front edge instead of k10.
Cont in pat as set until Front matches Back to markers, ending with a WS row. Mark side edge as beg of armhole.

Neck Shaping
Cont in pat *and at the same time* dec one st at end (front edge) of next and every foll 3rd row at same edge until 24 (26, 28) sts rem. Work even in pat until Front matches Back to shoulder, ending at side edge.

Shoulder Shaping
Bind off 12 (13, 14) sts at beg of next row and foll RS row.

RIGHT FRONT

Mark positions of buttons on Left Front, the first ½″ below first white stripe, the last one just below beg of neck shaping and the rem 2 equally spaced between.
Work Right Front as for Left Front, reversing shaping, working buttonholes when reached as given below and working first row of striped pat as foll:
1st row (RS) Using C, k7 (8, 7), [p1,

Dog motif

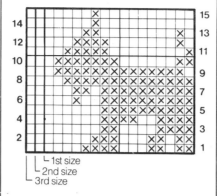

└ 1st size
└ 2nd size
└ 3rd size

k10] to end, ending last rep k7 (8, 7) instead of k10.
Buttonholes are worked as foll:
1st buttonhole row (RS) K3, bind off 2 sts, work in pat to end.
2nd buttonhole row Work in pat, casting on 2 sts over those bound off in last row.

SLEEVES

Using size 3 needles and A, cast on 49 sts. K 4 rows.
Change to size 6 needles, k one row and p one row. Place 3 dog motifs foll chart as foll:
1st row K1, *k2B, k1A, k2B, k3A, k4B, k4A, rep from * to end.
Cont in pat foll chart until 15 chart rows have been completed.
Using A, p one row, k one row.
Using C, p one row, inc 3 (5, 7) sts evenly across row. 52 (54, 56) sts.
Work in pat as for Back as foll:
1st row Using C, k9 (10, 11), [p1, k10] to end, ending last rep k9 (10, 11) instead of k10.
Cont in pat as set, inc one st at each end of every foll 4th row until there are 68 (74, 80) sts, working inc sts into pat as soon as possible.
Work even in pat until Sleeve measures 11 (12, 13)″ from beg.
Bind off.
Make 2nd Sleeve in same way.

COLLAR

Using size 6 needles and A, cast on 140 (144, 148) sts. Work 2 rows in k1, p1 rib.
Next 2 rows Rib to last 2 sts, turn.
Next 2 rows Rib to last 4 sts, turn.
Cont in this way working 2 sts less before turning at both ends until 30 rows have been worked from beg of shaping.

Next row Rib to end.
Next row Rib across all sts.
Bind off in rib.

FINISHING

Join shoulder seams. Sew Sleeves between markers.
Using size E crochet hook and C, work crochet chains along p ridges on RS of all pieces to form plaid pat. Join side and sleeve seams. With RS facing and using size 3 needles and A, pick up and k36 (40, 46) sts evenly along Right Front between cast-on edge and beg of neck shaping. K 4 rows. Bind off. Work border along Left Front in same way. Sew cast-on edge of Collar to neck edge, sewing first 4 row-ends to top of g st border. Sew on buttons.

PURSE

TO MAKE

Using size 6 needles and A, cast on 55 sts. K 4 rows.
Work in St st with g st border at each end as foll:
1st row (RS) K.
2nd row (WS) K 3, p to last 3 sts, k3.
Rep these 2 rows until Purse measures 2½″ from beg. Mark both ends of last row for top of flap. Cont as before until Back of Purse measures 6½″, ending with a WS row. Mark both ends of last row to indicate beg of Front. Rep first and 2nd rows 3 times more. Place 3 dog motifs on next row foll chart as foll:
1st row K4A, *k2B, k1A, k2B, k3A, k4B, k1A, rep from * to end, ending last rep k4A instead of k1A.
Break off B. Cont as before in A only until Purse Front measures 5″ ending, with a p row.
K 4 rows. Bind off.

FINISHING

Join side edges of Front and Back folding at lower markers. For cord using crochet hook and A double, make a length of ch 29½″ long. Then work 1sc in 2nd ch from hook, 1sc in each ch to end. Fasten off and sew to sides of Purse. Using A double, make a length of ch to fit button and sew to flap forming a loop. Sew on button.

It's Raining, It's Pouring

It's raining, it's pouring,
The old man's snoring;
He got into bed and bumped his head
And couldn't get up in the morning.

Child's Umbrella Sweater with Balaclava

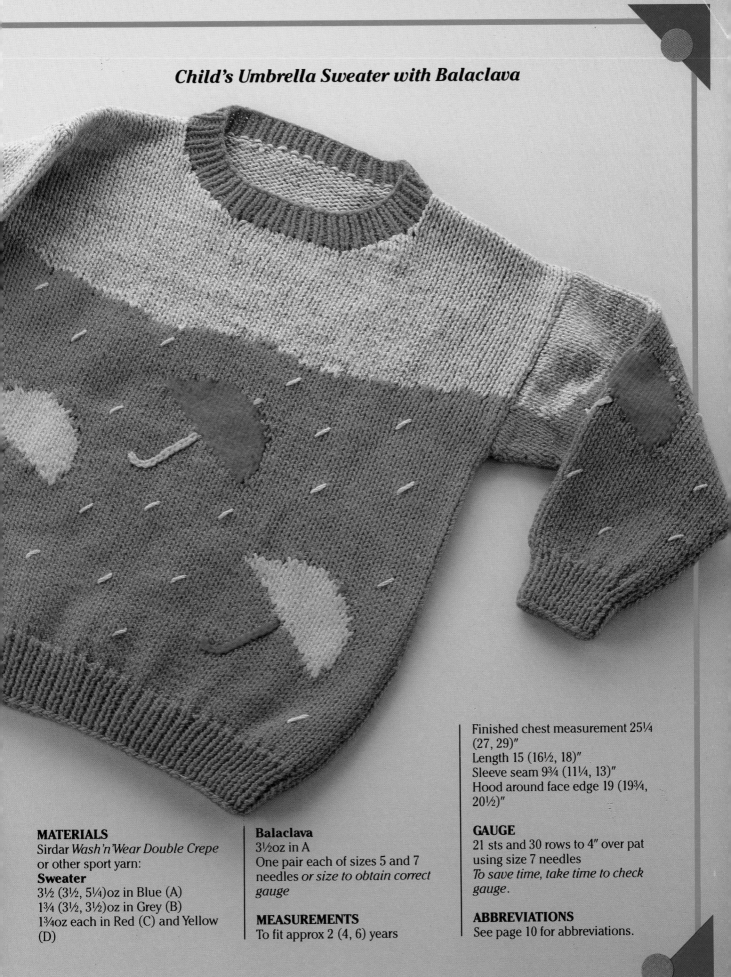

Finished chest measurement 25¼ (27, 29)"
Length 15 (16½, 18)"
Sleeve seam 9¾ (11¼, 13)"
Hood around face edge 19 (19¾, 20½)"

MATERIALS
Sirdar *Wash'n'Wear Double Crepe* or other sport yarn:
Sweater
3½ (3½, 5¼)oz in Blue (A)
1¾ (3½, 3½)oz in Grey (B)
1¾oz each in Red (C) and Yellow (D)

Balaclava
3½oz in A
One pair each of sizes 5 and 7 needles *or size to obtain correct gauge*

MEASUREMENTS
To fit approx 2 (4, 6) years

GAUGE
21 sts and 30 rows to 4" over pat using size 7 needles
To save time, take time to check gauge.

ABBREVIATIONS
See page 10 for abbreviations.

Sweater back and front

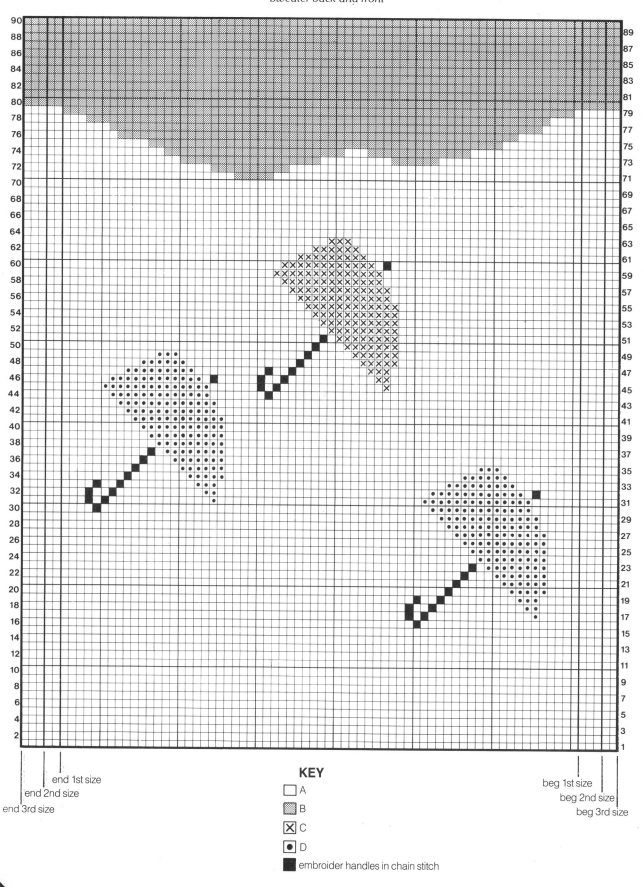

KEY

☐ A

▦ B

☒ C

⊡ D

◼ embroider handles in chain stitch

end 1st size
end 2nd size
end 3rd size

beg 1st size
beg 2nd size
beg 3rd size

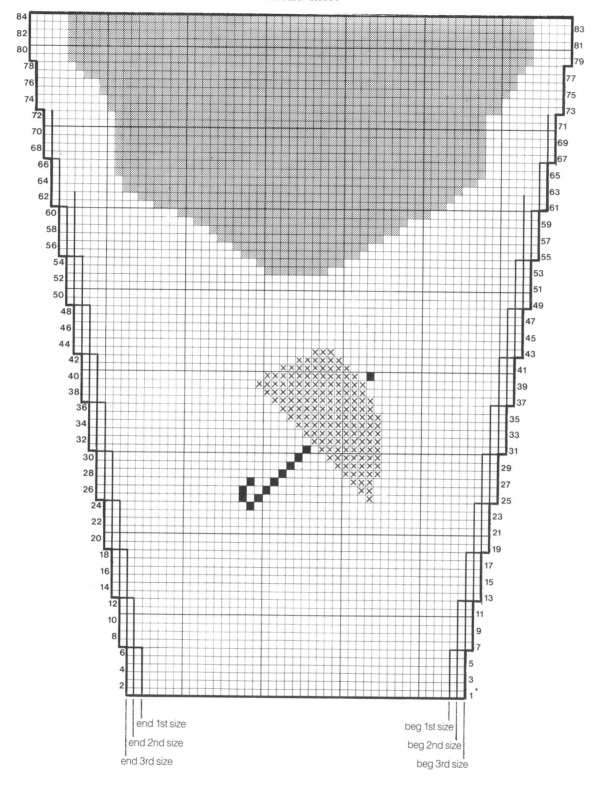

end 1st size

end 2nd size

end 3rd size

beg 1st size

beg 2nd size

beg 3rd size

SWEATER

BACK

Using size 5 needles and A, cast on 63 (68, 73) sts.

Work 1½ (1½, 1¾)″ in k1, p1 rib, inc 3 sts evenly across last row. 66 (71, 76) sts.

Change to size 7 needles and beg with a k row, work in St st, using a separate ball for each color, twisting yarn on WS when changing color to avoid holes, and reading k rows from right to left and p rows from left to right, until 79th chart row has been completed.**

Cont in St st and using B only, work even until Back measures 15 (16½, 18)″ from beg, ending with a WS row.

Shoulder Shaping

Cont in St st, bind off 6 (7, 8) sts at beg of next 4 rows and 7 sts at beg of foll 2 rows.

Slip rem 28 (29, 30) sts onto a st holder for back neck.

FRONT

Work as for back to **.

Cont in St st and using B only throughout, work even until Front measures 13½ (15, 16½)″ from beg, ending with a WS row.

Neck Shaping

Next row (RS) K27 (29, 31) and slip these sts onto a spare needle, k12 (13, 14) and leave these sts on a st holder, k27 (29, 31).

Cont on last set of sts only, dec one st at neck edge on next 8 rows. 19 (21, 23) sts.

Work even until Front measures same length as Back to shoulder, ending at armhole edge.

Shoulder Shaping

Bind off 6 (7, 8) sts at beg of next and foll WS row.

Work one row. Bind off rem 7 sts. With WS facing, rejoin yarn to neck edge of 27 (29, 31) sts on spare needle and complete to match first side, reversing shaping.

SLEEVES

Using size 5 needles and A, cast on 34 (36, 38) sts.

Work 1½ (1½, 1¾)″ in k1, p1 rib, ending with a RS row.

Cont in rib, inc 5 sts evenly across next row as foll:

Next row Rib 3 (4, 5), *insert tip of left-hand needle under horizontal strand before next st and work into back of it — called m1 —, rib 7, rep from * to last 3 (4, 5) sts, m1, rib to end. 39 (41, 43) sts.

Change to size 7 needles and work in St st foll chart, inc one st at each end of 7th and then every foll 6th row (as indicated on chart) until there are 57 (63, 69) sts, then work even in St st until 62nd (72nd, 84th) chart row has been completed.

Bind off.

Make 2nd Sleeve in same way.

EMBROIDERY

Using D for C umbrellas and C for D umbrellas, embroider chain stitch handle on umbrellas. Embroider tip of umbrellas in straight stitches, using same color as handle on each umbrella. Embroider rain in straight stitches as shown, using B.

NECKBAND

Join right shoulder seam.

Using size 5 needles and A, pick up and k17 sts down left front neck, k12 (13, 14) sts from centre front st holder, then pick up and k17 sts up right front neck, and k28 (29, 30) sts from back neck st holder inc 4 sts evenly across these back neck sts. 78 (80, 82) sts.

Work 7 rows in k1, p1 rib.

Bind off in rib.

FINISHING

Join left shoulder and neckband seams. Placing center of Sleeves at shoulder seam, sew bound-off edge of Sleeves to top part of Back and Front. Join side and sleeve seams.

BALACLAVA

TO MAKE

Using size 5 needles and A, cast on 82 (86, 90) sts.

Work 1″ in k1, p1 rib.

Change to size 7 needles and beg with a k row, work in St st until piece measures 3 (3¼, 3½)″ from beg, ending with a WS row.

Beg shaping on next row as foll:

Next row K6 and slip these sts onto a st holder, k to last 6 sts and slip these last sts onto a st holder. 70 (74, 78) sts.

Work even in St st until piece measures 9 (9½, 10)″ from beg, ending with a WS row.

Cont in St st throughout, bind off 21 (22, 23) sts at beg of next 2 rows.

Cont on center 28 (30, 32) sts for top, work even for 4 (4, 4¼)″.

Break off yarn and leave sts on a spare needle.

FRONT BAND

Sew sides of top to 21 (22, 23) bound-off sts at each side.

With RS facing and using size 5 needles, k6 from first st holder, pick up and k43 (45, 47) sts up right side of top, k 28 (30, 32) center sts from spare needle, pick up and k43 (45, 47) sts down left side of top, and rib across 6 sts of other st holder.

Work 7 rows in rib.

Bind off in rib.

FINISHING

Join front seam, including Front Band.

Jack and Jill

Jack and Jill went up the hill
To fetch a pail of water,
Jack fell down and broke his crown,
And Jill came tumbling after.

Child's Vest and Barrette or Bow Tie

MATERIALS
Wendy *Family Choice Dk* or other sport yarn:
Jill
3½oz in White (A)
1¾oz each in Pink (B), Light Green (C), Light Blue (D), and Light Yellow (E)
Jack
3½oz in Beige (A)

1¾oz each in Red (B), Green (C), Yellow (D), and Turquoise (E)
One pair each of sizes 3 and 6 needles *or size to obtain correct gauge*

MEASUREMENTS
To fit approx 2 (4, 6) years
Finished chest measurement 26 (28, 30)"

Length 13 (14½, 16)"

GAUGE
24 sts and 30 rows to 4" over pat using size 6 needles
To save time, take time to check gauge.

ABBREVIATIONS
See page 10 for abbreviations.

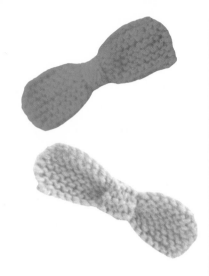

VEST

BACK

Using size 3 needles and A, cast on 72 (78, 84) sts. Work in k1, p1 rib for 13 rows, so ending with a RS row.
14th row (WS) * Rib 10 (11, 12), work in front and back of next st, rep from* 5 times more, rib to end. 78 (84, 90) sts.
Change to size 6 needles and beg with a k row, work in St st foll chart, rep rows 1-37 until Back measures 7½ (8¾, 10)" from beg, ending with a WS row.**

Armhole Shaping
Keeping pat correct as set throughout, bind off 4 sts at beg of next 2 rows. Dec one st at each end of next and foll 2 (3, 4) RS rows. 64 (68, 72) sts.
Work even until armholes measure 5½ (5¾, 6)", ending with a WS row.

Shoulder Shaping
Bind off 8 (9, 9) sts at beg of next 2 rows and 9 (9, 10) sts at beg of foll 2 rows. Leave rem 30 (32, 34) sts on a st holder for back neck.

FRONT

Work as for Back to**.

Armhole and Neck Shaping
Next row (RS) Bind off 4 sts, work 35 (38, 41) sts in pat, turn leaving rem sts on a spare needle.
Keeping pat correct as set throughout and cont on these sts only, work even for one row. Dec one st at each end of next and every

Sweater pattern

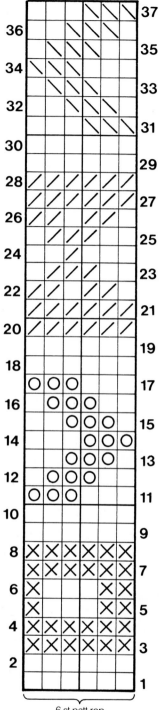

6 st patt rep

KEY

☐ = A
☒ = B
Ⓞ = C
▱ = D
◥ = E

other row 3 (4, 5) times in all.
Keeping armhole edge straight, cont dec one st at neck edge on every other row until 17 (18, 19) sts rem. Work even until armhole measures same as back armhole, ending at armhole edge. Bind off 8 (9, 9) sts at beg of next row, work one row, bind off 9 (9, 10) sts at beg of next row.
With RS facing, rejoin yarn to sts on spare needle and complete to match first side, reversing shaping.

NECKBAND

Join right shoulder seam. With RS facing and using size 3 needles and A, pick and k37 (39, 41) sts down left front neck, one st at center and k into back of it, 37 (39, 41) sts up right front neck, and k30 (32, 34) sts from back neck st holder. 105 (111, 117) sts.
1st row K1, *p1, k1, rep from * to end.
2nd and 4th rows Rib to 2 sts before center st, k2tog tbl, k1, k2tog, rib to end.
3rd and 5th rows Rib to center st, p1, rib to end.
Bind off in rib working decs as for 2nd row while binding off.

ARMBANDS

Join left shoulder seam. With RS facing, using size 3 needles and A, pick up and k76 (80, 84) sts evenly around armhole.
Work in k1, p1 rib for 5 rows.
Bind off in rib.

FINISHING

Join side seams.

BOW TIE AND BARRETTE

TO MAKE

Using size 3 needles and B or C, cast on 18 sts and work in g st for 12 rows. Bind off. Cast on 4 sts and work 12 rows in St st for band. Bind off.

FINISHING

Fold band around center and sew at back. Sew to tip of V-neck for bow tie and to a barrette for hair accessory.

Here We Go Round
the Mulberry Bush

Here we go round the mulberry bush,
The mulberry bush, the mulberry bush,
Here we go round the mulberry bush,
On a cold and frosty morning.

Child's Jacket, Helmet, and Mittens

MATERIALS

Hayfield *Grampion Chunky* or other bulky yarn:
14 (15¾, 17½)oz in Brown (A)
1¾oz in Cream (B)
12 (14, 16)″ open-ended zipper
4 small buttons
One pair each of sizes 9 and 10½ needles *or size to obtain correct gauge*

MEASUREMENTS

To fit approx 2 (4, 6) years
Finished chest measurement 30¼ (31½, 33¾)″
Length 14 (16, 18)″
Sleeve seam 10½ (11½, 12½)″

GAUGE

14 sts and 22 rows to 4″ over pat using size 10½ needles
To save time, take time to check gauge.

ABBREVIATIONS

See page 10 for abbreviations.

JACKET

BACK

Using size 9 needles and A, cast on 47 (47, 52) sts.
1st rib row (RS) K2, *p3, k2, rep from * to end.
2nd rib row P2, *k3, p2, rep from * to end.
Rep these 2 rib rows 4 times more, inc 6 (8, 7) sts evenly across last row. 53 (55, 59) sts.
Change to size 10½ needles and seed st pat as foll:
1st pat row K1, *p1, k1, rep from * to end.
Rep first pat row throughout until Back measures 14 (16, 18)″ from beg, ending with a WS row.

Shoulder Shaping
Keeping pat correct, bind off 19 (19, 20) sts at beg of next 2 rows.
Leave rem 15 (17, 19) sts on a st holder for back neck.

LEFT FRONT

Using size 9 needles and A, cast on

22 (22, 27) sts.
Work 10 rows in rib as for Back, inc 3 (5, 2) sts evenly across last row. 25 (27, 29) sts.
Change to size 10½ needles and work in pat as for Back until Front measures 12 (14, 15½)″ from beg, ending with a RS row.

Neck Shaping
Keeping pat correct throughout, bind off 4 (5, 6) sts at beg of next row.
Dec one st at neck edge on next and every foll RS row until 19 (19, 20) sts rem.
Work even until Front measures same as Back to shoulders, ending with a WS row.
Bind off.

RIGHT FRONT

Work as for Left Front, reversing shaping.

SLEEVES

Using size 9 needles and A, cast on 27 sts.
Work 8 rows in rib as for Back, inc 0 (2, 4) sts evenly across last row. 27 (29, 31) sts.
Change to size 10½ needles and cont in seed st pat as for Back, inc one st at each end of 5th and every foll 4th row until there are 43 (47, 51) sts.
Work even in pat until Sleeve measures 10½ (11½, 12½)″ from beg, ending with a WS row.
Bind off.
Make 2nd Sleeve in same way.

COLLAR

Join shoulder seams.
Using size 9 needles and B and with RS facing, pick up and k21 (22, 23) sts evenly up right front neck, k15 (17, 19) back neck sts from holder, then pick up and k21 (22, 23) sts evenly down left front neck. 57 (61, 65) sts.
Next 2 rows K1, *p1, k1, rep from * to end.
Next row K1, k2tog, work in pat as set to last 3 sts, k2tog, k1.

Work 3 (3½, 4)″ in seed st as set, *and at the same time* dec one st at each end of every foll 4th row until 49 (53, 57) sts rem, ending with a WS row.
With RS facing, pick up and k13 (14, 15) sts evenly along shaped edge of Collar, p49 (53, 57) sts which were left, then pick up and k13 (14, 15) sts evenly along other shaped edge of collar.
Bind off.

POCKET TOPS

Using size 9 needles and B, cast on 14 sts.
1st rib row (RS) P1, *k2, p3, rep from * to last 3 sts, k2, p1.
2nd rib row K1, *p2, k3, rep from * to last 3 sts, p2, k1.
Rep these 2 rib rows twice more.
Bind off in rib.

EPAULETTES

Using size 9 needles and B, cast on 15 (17, 19) sts.
1st row (RS) K1 *p1, k1, rep from * to end.
2nd row P1 and k1 both into first st, work in seed st to end as set.
3rd row Work in seed st to last st, p1 and k1 both into last st.
4th row P2tog, work in seed st to end.
5th row Work in seed st to last 2 sts, k2tog.
6th row Work in seed st to end.
Bind off in pat.

FINISHING

Sew on Sleeves with center of bound-off edge of Sleeve at shoulder seam.
Join side and sleeves seams. Sew one epaulette to each shoulder.
Sew pocket tops in place for mock pockets.
Sew in zipper.
Sew one button to end of each epaulette.

HELMET

TO MAKE

Using size 10½ needles and A, cast

on 65 (67, 69) sts.
Work 24 (26, 28) rows in seed st pat as for Back of Jacket.

Top Shaping
Next row Work 5 (5, 3) sts in pat, k3tog, *work 10 (8, 7) sts in pat, k3tog, rep from * to last 5 (4, 3) sts, work in pat to end. 55 sts.
Work even for 5 rows.
Next row Work 2 sts in pat, k3tog, [work 3 sts in pat, k3tog] 8 times, work in pat to end.
Work even for 3 rows.
Next row Work one st in pat, k3tog, [work one st in pat, k3tog] 8 times, work rem st in pat.
Work even for one row.
Next row K1, [k2tog] 9 times. 10 sts.
Break off yarn, thread through rem sts and pull tightly.
Fasten off.

EAR FLAPS
Using size 10½ needles and A, cast on 13 sts.
Work 11 rows in seed st pat as for Back of Jacket.
Next row Work 2 sts in pat, k3tog, work 3 sts in pat, k3tog, work 2 sts in pat. 9 sts.
Work even for one row.
Next row Work 3 sts in pat, k3tog, work 3 sts in pat.
Work even for one row.
Next row Work 2 sts in pat, k3tog, work 2 sts in pat.
Work even for one row.
Next row Work 3 sts in pat, k2tog. 4 sts.
Work even in pat until Flap measures 6″ from beg.
Next row [P2tog] twice.
Next row K2tog.
Fasten off.

FINISHING
Join helmet seam. Sew cast-on edge of ear flaps to cast-on edge of helmet.
Sew 2 buttons to one end of the strap, lay the other end of the strap over buttons and fasten through the knitting.

MITTENS

TO MAKE
Using size 9 needles and B, cast on 22 (27, 27) sts. Work 3″ in rib as for Back of Jacket, ending with a first rib row.
Break off B. Change to size 10½ needles and A.
Next row P to end, inc 3 (0, 2) sts evenly across row. 25 (27, 29) sts.
Work 4 rows in seed st pat as for Back of Jacket.

Thumb Shaping
Next row Work 12 (13, 14) sts in pat, insert tip of left-hand needle under horizontal strand before next st and work into back of it — called m1 —, k1, m1, work in pat to end.
Next row Work 12 (13, 14) sts in pat, p3, work in pat to end.
Next row Work 12 (13, 14) sts in pat, m1, k3, m1, work in pat to end.
Next row Work 12 (13, 14) sts in pat, p5, work in pat to end.
Next row Work 12 (13, 14) sts in pat, m1, k5, m1, work in pat to end.
Next row Work 12 (13, 14) sts in pat, p7, work in pat to end.
Next row Work 12 (13, 14) sts in pat, m1, k7, m1, work in pat to end.
Next row Work 12 (13, 14) sts in pat, p9, work in pat to end.
Next row Work 12 (13, 14) sts in pat, m1, k9, m1, turn leaving rem sts on a spare needle.

Next row P11, turn leaving rem sts on a spare needle.
Work 5 (7, 9) rows in St st as set on these 11 sts.
Next row P1, *p2 tog, rep from * to end. 6 sts.
Break off yarn, thread through sts, pull tightly and fasten off. Join thumb seam.
Return to sts on spare needle and with RS facing, rejoin yarn and work in pat to end.

Join Pieces
Next row Work in pat to end, pick up and k1 st from base of thumb, then with WS facing, work in pat to end across sts which were left. 25 (27, 29) sts.
Work even in pat until piece measures 6½ (7, 7½)″ from beg, ending with a WS row.

Top Shaping
Next row K1, *p2tog, rep from * to end. 13 (14, 15) sts.
Next row K1 (0, 1), *p2tog, rep from * to end. 7 (7, 8) sts.
Break off yarn, thread through sts, pull tightly and fasten off.
Make 2nd Mitten in same way.

FINISHING
Join mitten seam.

Curly Locks! Curly Locks!

Curly locks! Curly locks! Wilt thou be mine?
Thou shalt not wash dishes, nor yet feed the swine;
But sit on a cushion and sew a fine seam,
And feed upon strawberries, sugar, and cream!

Girl's Lacy Sweater And Doll

Girl's Lacy Sweater and Doll

MATERIALS

Patons *Venus* or other sport yarn:
8¾oz in Blue (A)
Small amount each in Pink (B),
Black (C), and Red (D)
1yd of narrow blue ribbon
Lace collar for sweater
Stuffing for doll
Floral fabric, matching thread,
lace, and ribbon for doll's dress
One pair each of sizes 6 and 8
needles *or size to obtain correct
gauge*
Size G crochet hook

MEASUREMENTS

To fit approx 4-6 years (one size)
Finished chest measurement 29¼"
Length 15"

GAUGE

20 sts and 22 rows to 4½" over pat
using size 8 needles
*To save time, take time to check
gauge.*

ABBREVIATIONS

See page 10 for abbreviations.

SWEATER

BACK

Using size 6 needles and A, cast on
65 sts. Work 2½" in k1, p1 rib,
ending with a WS row.
Change to size 8 needles and work
pat as foll:
1st row (RS) K1, p1, *k3, p1, rep
from * to last 3 sts, k3.
2nd row P3, *k1, p3, rep from * to
last 2 sts, k1, p1.
3rd row As first row.
4th row K1, p2tog, *yo, k1, yo,
p3tog, rep from * to last 2 sts, yo, k2.
5th row K3, *p1, k3, rep from * to
last 2 sts, p1, k1.
6th row P1, k1, *p3, k1, rep from *
to last 3 sts, p3.
7th row As 5th row.
8th row K2, yo, *p3tog, yo, k1, yo,
rep from * to last 3 sts, p2tog, k1.
These 8 rows form the pat and are
rep throughout.
Cont in pat until Back measures 9"
from beg, ending with a WS row.

Armhole Shaping
Keeping pat correct throughout,

bind off 2 sts at beg of next 2 rows.
Dec one st at beg of next 2 rows. 59
sts.
Work even until armhole measures
5", ending with a WS row.

Neck Shaping
Next row Work 18 sts in pat, turn
leaving rem sts on a spare needle.
Cont on these sts only, dec one st at
neck edge on next and foll 2 WS
rows.
Bind off rem 15 sts.
Return to rem sts and with RS
facing, rejoin yarn and bind off
center 23 sts, work in pat to end of
row.
Complete to match first side,
reversing shaping.

FRONT
Work as for Back.

SLEEVES
Using size 6 needles and A, cast on
44 sts.
Work in k1, p1 rib for 4 rows, inc
one st at end of last row. 45 sts.
Change to size 8 needles and work
in pat as for Back until Sleeve
measures 5¾" from beg, ending
with a WS row.

Cap Shaping.
Bind off 2 sts at beg of next 2 rows,
then bind off one st at beg of every
row until 27 sts rem.
Bind off.
Make 2nd Sleeve in same way.

NECK EDGING
Join neck and side seams.
Using size G crochet hook and A
and beg at right shoulder, work one
round of sc around neck edge.
Fasten off.

FINISHING
Join Sleeve seams, then set Sleeves
in armholes. Sew collar to neck
and thread narrow ribbon through
knitted fabric at waist.

DOLL

BODY
Using size 6 needles and B, cast on
26 sts.

Work 10 rows in St st.
Cont in St st throughout, dec one st
at each end of next and every foll
4th row until 12 sts rem.
Bind off 3 sts at beg of next 2 rows.
6 sts.
Inc one st at each end of next row. 8
sts.
Work even for 10 rows.
Dec one st at each end of next row.
Bind off rem 6 sts.
Make 2nd piece in same way.

ARMS
Using size 6 needles and B, cast on
36 sts.
K 11 rows in St st. Bind off.
Make 2nd Arm in same way.

FINISHING
Sew 2 body pieces tog, leaving an
opening at lower edge. Stuff firmly
and close opening. Fold Arms in
half lengthwise and sew tog,
leaving an opening at one end.
Stuff Arms and sew to Body. Using
C, embroider eyes. Using D,
embroider mouth.
Sew lengths of C to doll's head for
hair and secure at the back in a
bun, using D to tie a bow.

Hat
Cut out two circles 4" in diameter
from floral fabric.
With RS tog, sew the two pieces
tog, allowing a ½" seam and
leaving an opening. Turn right side
out and sew the opening to close it.
Work a row of gathering stitches ½"
from edge of Hat.
Place Hat on doll's head and pull
gathering thread to fit head. Secure
in place with a few stitches.

Dress
Cut two pieces of floral fabric 8½"
by 7".
With RS tog, sew one of shorter
sides tog leaving 1" open at center
for neck. Sew longer sides tog,
leaving ¾" open for armholes. Turn
right side out.
Sew a length of lace to hem of
dress.
Put dress on doll and secure in
place with a length of narrow
ribbon at the waist.

The Queen of Hearts

The Queen of Hearts
She made some tarts,
All on a summer's day;
The Knave of Hearts
He stole those tarts,
And took them clean away.

Heart Dress and Purse

MATERIALS

Robin *Feelings DK* or other sport yarn:
7 (10½)oz in White (A)
3½oz in Pink (B)
4 buttons
1 yd of 1½" wide pink ribbon
One pair each of sizes 8 and 9 needles *or size to obtain correct gauge*
Size E crochet hook

MEASUREMENTS

To fit approx 4 (6) years
Finished chest measurement 25 (26¾)"
Length 20½ (24)"

GAUGE

18 sts and 22 rows to 4" over St st using size 9 needles
To save time, take time to check gauge.

ABBREVIATIONS

See page 10 for abbreviations.

DRESS

BACK

Using size 8 needles and A, cast on 112 (120) sts. Work 3 rows in g st. Change to size 9 needles and beg with a k row, work 6 rows in St st, so ending with a WS row.
Cont in St st, foll chart from chart row 1 (k row) until 28th chart row has been completed. Cont foll chart, rep rows 1-28, until Skirt measures 11½ (13¾) " from beg, ending with a RS row.
Next row *P2tog, rep from * to end. 56 (60) sts.**
K one row.

Bodice Back
Next row P28 (30) sts, turn leaving rem sts on a spare needle.
Cont on these sts only work as foll:
Next row Cast on 3 sts, k to end. 31 (33) sts.
Next row P to last 3 sts, k3.
Working the 3 border sts in g st, cont in St st for 2 rows, so ending with a WS row. Cont in St st, foll bodice chart from row 1, rep rows 1-28 until Back measures 15½ (18½)", ending with a RS row.

Armhole Shaping
Keeping to chart pat throughout, bind off 2 sts at beg of next row. Work even for one row. Dec one st at armhole edge on next 3 rows. 26 (28) sts.
Work even until armhole measures 5(5½)", ending with a RS row.
Bind off 7 (8) sts at beg of next and foll WS row. Bind off rem 12 sts.
Mark position of 4 buttons along back opening, the first ½" below neck edge and rem 3 equally spaced below.
Return to sts on spare needle and with WS facing, cast on 3 sts, k3, p to end. Complete to match first side, reversing shaping and working buttonholes as foll:
Buttonhole row Work in pat to last 4 sts, k2tog, yo, k2.

FRONT

Work as given for Back to **.
Cont in St st and beg with a k row, work even for 6 rows. Cont in St st, foll bodice chart from row 1, rep rows 1-28 until Front measures 15½ (18½)" ending with a WS row.

Armhole Shaping
Keeping to chart pat throughout, bind off 2 sts at beg of next 2 rows. Dec one st at each end of next 3 rows. 46 (50) sts. Work even until armholes measure 3 (3½)", ending with a WS row.

Neck Shaping
Next row K18 (20) sts and slip these onto a spare needle, bind off 10 sts, k to end.
Cont on these sts only, dec one st at neck edge on next 4 rows 14 (16) sts. Work until armhole measures same as Back, ending with a RS row.

Shoulder Shaping
Bind off 7 (8) sts at beg of next and foll WS row. Return to sts on spare needle and complete to match first side, reversing shaping.

SLEEVES

Using size 8 needles and A, cast on 92 (100) sts. Work 4 rows in g st.
Next row *K2tog, rep from * to end. 46 (50) sts.
Change to size 9 needles and beg with a k row, work 6 rows in St st, so ending with a WS row.
Cont in St st, foll sleeve chart from row 1, rep rows 1-28 until Sleeve measures 2½ (3)" from beg, ending with a WS row.

Cap Shaping
Keeping to pat throughout, bind off 2 sts at beg of next 2 rows. Dec one st at each end of next row and then every other row until 26 sts rem. Dec one st at each end of every row until 10 sts rem. Cast off.
Make 2nd Sleeve in same way.

COLLAR

Using size 8 needles and A, cast on 32 (34) sts.
Pat row K3, *yo, sl1-k1-psso, rep from * to last 3 sts, k3.
Rep pat row until Collar measures 1¼". Change to size 9 needles and cont in pat until Collar measures 2½ (3)". Work 3 rows in g st. Bind off loosely.

FINISHING

Join shoulder seams. Set in Sleeves. Join side and sleeve seams. Sew on Collar and buttons. Tie ribbon around waist.

PURSE

TO MAKE

Using size 8 needles and B, cast on 3 sts. Beg with a k row, work in St st, inc one st at each end of 3rd and every foll RS row until there are 25 sts. Work even for 3 rows.

Top Shaping
Next row K11 sts, bind off 3 sts, k to end.
Cont on last set of sts, dec one st at each end of every row until 3 sts rem. Bind off. With WS facing, rejoin yarn to first set of sts and complete to match first side.
Make 2nd piece in same way.

FINISHING

Join side seams. Work one row of sc around top edge. Make a crochet chain for strap and sew in position.

Skirt chart

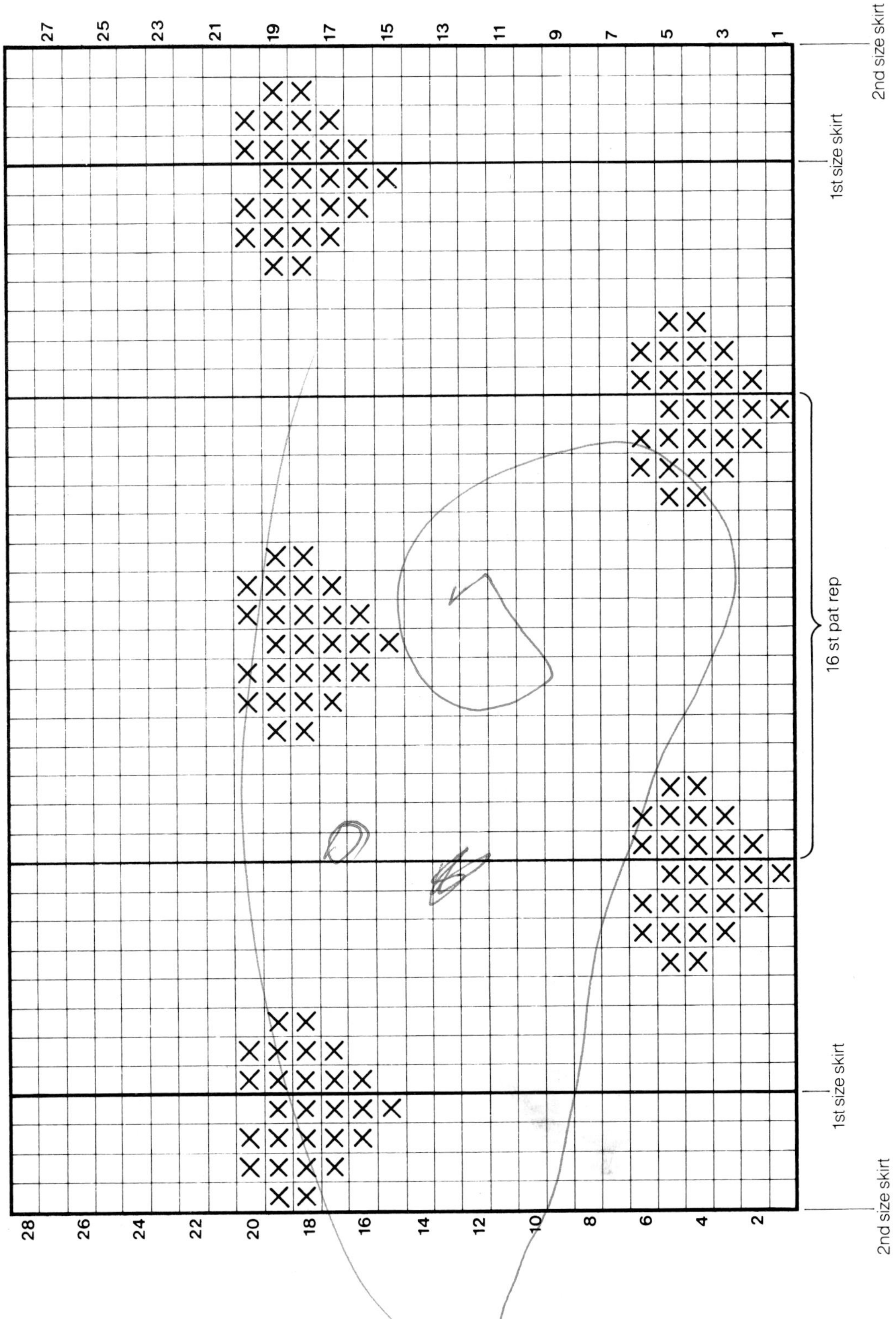

27 25 23 21 19 17 15 13 11 9 7 5 3 1
28 26 24 22 20 18 16 14 12 10 8 6 4 2
2nd size skirt
1st size skirt
16 st pat rep
1st size skirt
2nd size skirt

KEY

☐ =A

☒ =B

Bodice chart

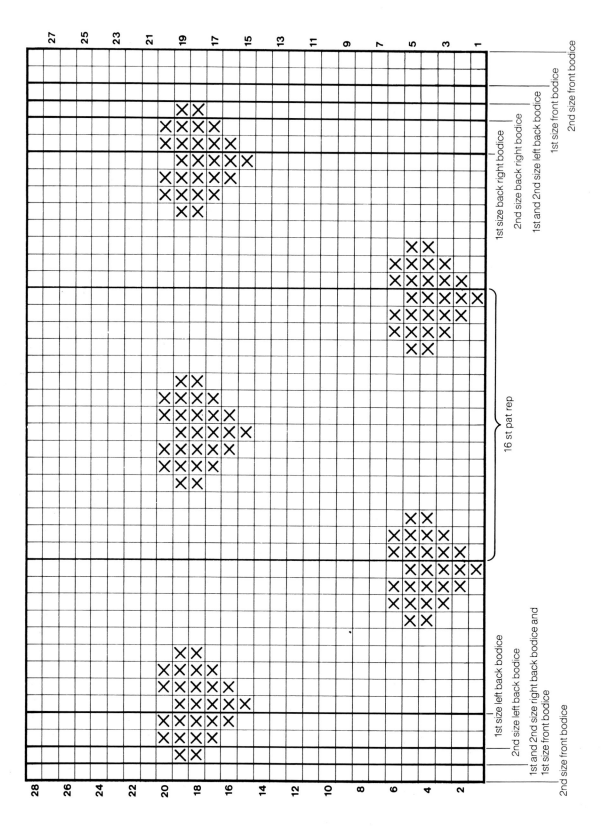

16 st pat rep

1st size back right bodice
2nd size back right bodice
1st and 2nd size left back bodice
1st size front bodice
2nd size front bodice

1st size left back bodice
2nd size left back bodice
1st and 2nd size right back bodice and
1st size front bodice
2nd size front bodice

Sleeve chart

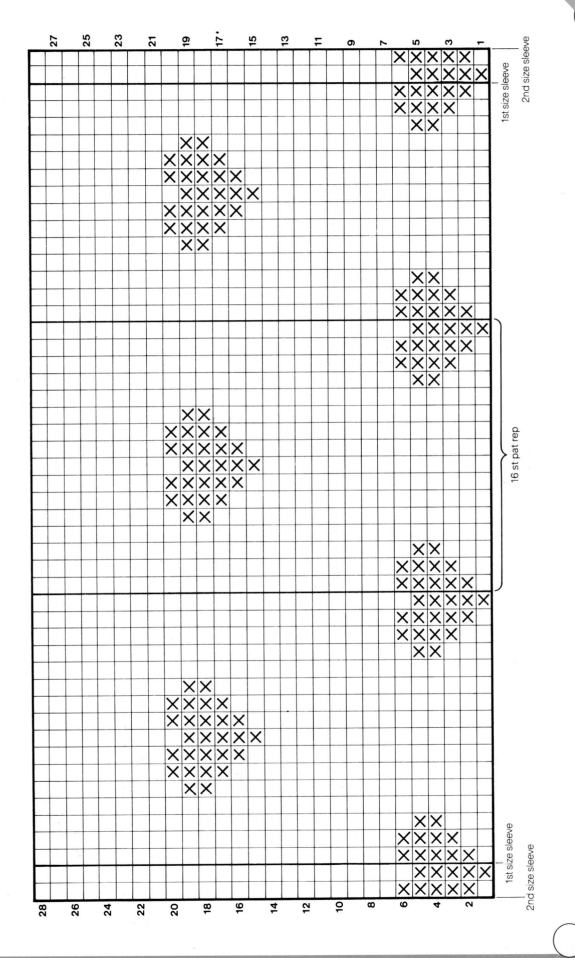

Round and Round the Garden

Round and round the garden,
Like a teddy bear;
One step, two step,
Tickle you under there!

Sweater and Hand Puppet

MATERIALS
Pingouin *Pingofrance* or other
sport yarn:
8¾ (10½, 12¼)oz in Cream (A)
3½oz in Gold (C)
1¾oz each in Burgundy (B) and
Green (E)
Small amounts each in Brown (D),
Pink (F), and Purple (G)
2 small buttons

Stuffing and narrow brown ribbon
One pair each of sizes 3 and 5
needles *or size to obtain correct
gauge*

MEASUREMENTS
To fit approx 2 (4, 6) years
Finished chest measurement 24¾
(26, 27¼)"
Length 13½ (14, 14½)"

Sleeve seam 8 (8½, 9)"

GAUGE
24 sts and 28 rows to 4" over St st
using size 5 needles
*To save time, take time to check
gauge.*

ABBREVIATIONS
See page 10 for abbreviations.

125

SWEATER

BACK

Using size 3 needles and A, cast on 70 (74, 78) sts.
Work in k1, p1 rib for 1½", inc 4 sts evenly across last row. 74 (78, 82) sts.**

Change to size 5 needles and beg stripe pat as foll:
1st row (RS) With A, k.
2nd row With A, p.
3rd-18th rows Rep last 2 rows 8 times more.
19th row With B, k.
20th row With B, p.
These 20 rows form the stripe pat. Rep them once more and first 4 (8, 12) rows again.

Armhole Shaping

Cont in stripe pat until 3rd B stripe from beg has been worked, then working in St st throughout, cont with A only *and at the same time* bind off 3 sts at beg of next 2 rows, 2 sts at beg of next 4 rows, then dec one st at each end of every other row 4 times. 52 (56, 60) sts.
Work even until Back measures 13½ (14, 14½)" from beg, ending with a WS row.

Shoulder and Neck Shaping

Bind off 5 sts at beg of next 2 rows.
Next row Bind off 5 (5, 6) sts, k7 (9, 10) sts and slip these sts onto a spare needle, bind off 18 (18, 18) sts, k to end.
Cont on last set of 12 (14, 16) sts, bind off 5 (5, 6) sts at beg of next row and 3 (3, 4) sts at neck edge on next row.
Bind off rem 4 (6, 6) sts.
With WS facing, rejoin A to neck edge of the 7 (9, 10) sts on spare needle, bind off 3 (3, 4) sts, p to end.
Bind off rem 4 (6, 6) sts.

FRONT

Work as for Back to **.
Change to size 5 needles and beg with a k row, work in St st foll chart until 76th row has been completed, working armhole shaping as indicated. 52 (56, 60) sts.
Cont in St st throughout and using A only, work even for 3 (5, 7) rows, so ending with a WS row.

Neck and Shoulder Shaping

Next row K22 (22, 26) sts and slip these onto a spare needle, bind off 8 (8, 8) sts, k to end.
Cont on 22 (24, 26) sts, work even for one row. Bind off 3 (3, 4) sts at beg (neck edge) of next row, 2 sts at same edge on next 2 RS rows, and one st on next RS row, so ending at armhole edge. Bind off 5 (5, 5) sts at beg of next row and 5 (5, 6) sts on foll WS row. Work even for one row. Bind off rem 4 (6, 6) sts.
With WS facing, rejoin A to neck edge of sts on spare needle, bind off 3 sts at beg of next row and foll WS row, 2 (2, 3) sts at same edge of next WS row, so ending at armhole edge.
Work shoulder shaping as for first side, reversing shaping.

SLEEVES

Using size 3 needles and A, cast on 32 (36, 40) sts. Work in k1, p1 rib for 1½", inc 9 (11, 13) sts evenly across last row. 41 (47, 53) sts.
Change to size 5 needles and cont in stripe pat as for Back, inc one st at each end of 7th row and every foll 8th row until there are 51 (57, 63) sts.
Cont in pat throughout, work even until Sleeve measures 8½ (8½, 9)" from beg, ending with a WS row.

Cap Shaping

Bind off 3 sts at beg of next 2 rows, 2 sts at beg of next 4 rows, one st at beg of next 8 (12, 16) rows, then 2 sts at beg of foll 2 rows, 3 sts at beg of next 2 rows and 5 sts at beg of next 2 rows. 9 (11, 13) sts. Bind off.
Make 2nd Sleeve in same way.

NECKBAND

Join right shoulder seam.
Using size 3 needles and A and with RS facing, pick up and k40 (44, 46) sts around front neck edge and 30 (30, 32) sts across back neck. 70 (74, 78) sts. Work 4 rows in k1, p1 rib.
Bind off in rib.

SHOULDER BANDS

Using size 3 needles and A and with RS facing, pick up and k20 (22, 24) sts across left front shoulder, including edge of neckband.
Work one row in k1, p1 rib.
1st buttonhole row (RS) Rib 6 (7, 8), bind off one st, rib 6 (7, 8), bind off one st, rib to end.
2nd buttonhole row Work in rib, casting on one st over those bound off.
Rib one row more. Bind off in rib.
Work Band on left back shoulder in same way, but omitting buttonholes.

FINISHING

Place left front shoulder Band over back Band and sew along side edges. Work embroidery foll chart. Set in Sleeves. Join sleeve and side seams. Sew 2 buttons on left back shoulder Band to correspond with buttonholes.

TEDDY PUPPET

BODY

Using size 3 needles and C, cast on 36 sts. Work 2 rows in k1, p1 rib.
Change to size 5 needles and beg with a k row, work 36 rows in St st.
Cont in St st throughout, shape arms by casting on 4 sts at beg of next 2 rows. 44 sts.
Work even for 6 rows. Bind off 18 sts at beg of next 2 rows.
Work even for 2 rows.
Make 2nd piece in same way.

Head

Inc one st at each end of next row and then every other row until there are 14 sts. Work even for 5 rows, ending with a WS row. Dec one st at each end of next and every foll RS row until there are 8 sts.
P one row. Bind off.

EARS

Using size 5 needles and C, cast on 9 sts. Beg with a k row, work 2 rows in St st. Cont in St st throughout, dec one st at each end of next and foll 2 RS rows. 3 sts. P one row.
Inc one st at each end of next row and foll 2 RS rows. 9 sts.
P one row. Bind off.
Make 2nd Ear in same way.

MUZZLE

Using size 5 needles and C, cast on 21 sts. Beg with a k row, work 2 rows in St st.

Sweater front

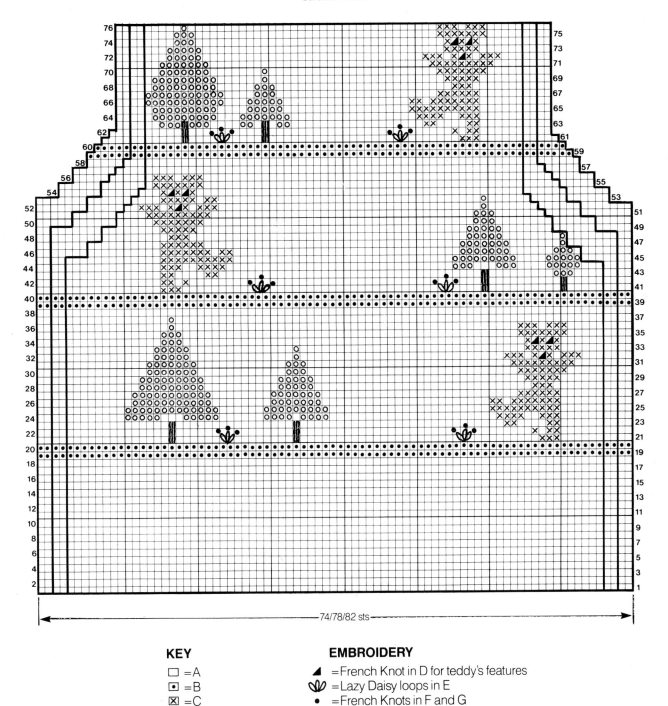

— 74/78/82 sts —

KEY

□ = A
· = B
☒ = C
▥ = D
◙ = E

EMBROIDERY

◢ = French Knot in D for teddy's features
❦ = Lazy Daisy loops in E
• = French Knots in F and G

Next row K2, [k3tog, k4] twice, k3tog, k2. P one row.
Next row K1, [k3tog, k2] twice, k3tog, k1.
Break off yarn, thread through 9 sts, pull tightly and join seam. Stuff firmly and sew in place.

PAWS
Join shoulder and arm seams. Using size 5 needles and C and with RS facing, pick up and k14 sts along row ends of arms. Work 4 rows in g st. Cont in g st, dec one st at each end of next 3 rows. Bind off.

FINISHING
Join paw and side seams. Using D, embroider eyes, nose, and mouth as shown. Join head seam and stuff head.
Tie a ribbon round neck. Join ear seam, stuff and sew in place.

Yarn Addresses

COPLEY
P.O. Box 46,
Darlington,
Co. Durham,
Great Britain

Copley Inc.
6900 South Point Drive,
Jacksonville,
Florida 32216, U.S.A.

EMU
Leeds Road,
Greengates,
Bradford,
West Yorkshire,
England

Plymouth Yarn Co,
P.O. Box 28,
500 Lafayette Street,
Bristol,
Pennsylvania 19007, U.S.A.

Karingal,
Vic/Tas. P.T.Y. Ltd.
6 Macro Court,
Rowville,
Victoria 3178, Australia

PINGOUIN
French Wools Ltd,
Station House,
81-83 Fulham High Street,
London SW6 3JW,
England

HAYFIELD
Hayfield Textiles Ltd,
Hayfield Mills,
Glusburn,
Keighley,
West Yorkshire BD20 8QP,
England

Cascade Yarns Inc,
204, 3rd Avenue South,
Seattle,
Washington 981041, U.S.A.

Panda Yarns P.T.Y. Ltd,
17–27 Brunswick Road,
East Brunswick 3057,
Victoria, Australia

PATONS
Patons & Baldwin Ltd,
Macmullen Road,
Darlington,
Co. Durham DL1 1YQ,
Great Britain

Susan Bates, Inc,
212 Middlesex Avenue,
Chester,
Connecticut 06412, U.S.A.

Coats Patons Ltd,
321-355 Ferntree Gulley Road,
PO Box 110,
Mount Waverley,
Victoria 3149, Australia

ROBIN
Robin Mills,
Idle,
Bradford,
West Yorkshire,
England

Plymouth Yarn Co,
P.O. Box 28,
500 Lafayette Street,
Bristol,
Pennsylvania 19007, U.S.A.

The Needlewoman,
Karingal Grove,
Huon,
Tasmania 3066, Australia

SIRDAR
Sirdar PLC,
Flanshaw Lane,
Alverthorpe,
Wakefield,
W. Yorkshire WF2 9ND,
England

Kendex Corporation,
31332 Cia Colinas,
107 West Lake Village,
California 91362, U.S.A.

Diamond Yarns Corporation,
153 Bridgeland Avenue,
Unit 11,
Toronto,
Ontario M6A 2Y6, Canada

SPECTRUM
Spectrum Yarns Ltd,
Bankwell Road,
Milnsbridge,
Huddersfield,
West Yorkshire HD3 4LU,
England

SUNBEAM
Richard Ingham & Co Ltd,
Crawshaw Mills,
Pudsey, Yorkshire,
England

TWILLEYS
H.G. Twilleys Ltd,
Roman Mill, Stamford,
Lincoln PE9 1BG,
England

Leon Summers,
456 South Norton Avenue,
Los Angeles,
California 90020, U.S.A.

S.R. Kertzer Ltd,
257 Adelaide Street,
W. Toronto,
Ontario M5H 1Y1, Canada

Panda Yarns P.T.Y. Ltd,
17 – 27 Brunswick Road,
East Brunswick 3057,
Victoria, Australia

WENDY
Carter & Parker Ltd,
Gordon Mills,
Guiseley,
West Yorkshire,
England

White Buffalo Mills Ltd,
545 Assiniboine Av,
Brandon,
Manitoba, Canada

Cruft Warehouse,
30 Guess Av,
Arncliffe,
New South Wales 2205,
Australia

House of Settler,
2120 Broadway,
Lubbock,
Texas 79401, U.S.A.